SCIENTIFIC LECTURES

SCIENTIFIC LECTURES

BY THE RIGHT HON.

SIR JOHN LUBBOCK

Essay Index Reprint Series

BOOKS FOR LIBRARIES PRESS
FREEPORT, NEW YORK

First Published 1879
Reprinted 1972

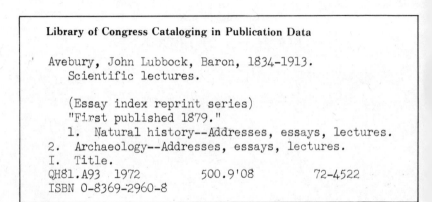

Library of Congress Cataloging in Publication Data

Avebury, John Lubbock, Baron, 1834-1913.
    Scientific lectures.

    (Essay index reprint series)
    "First published 1879."
    1. Natural history--Addresses, essays, lectures.
2. Archaeology--Addresses, essays, lectures.
I. Title.
QH81.A93 1972   500.9'08   72-4522
ISBN 0-8369-2960-8

PRINTED IN THE UNITED STATES OF AMERICA

PREFACE.

In these days of limited leisure, and continually increasing literary activity, when there is more and more that every intelligent man would wish to read, and apparently less and less time for reading, an apology is required for the publication of a book, however small, which does not profess to contain anything absolutely new. At the same time, the very circumstances above referred to, render it desirable that the observations of specialists should be condensed and epitomized for the general reader, and hence the continually increasing demand for lectures; which need not, because they are popular, be the less truly scientific.

The fact that the present book does not contain anything new to those who have specially studied the parts of science with which it deals, precludes it from constituting any tax on the time of those who have devoted themselves to these subjects.

On the other hand, I hope it may be found to present the facts in a condensed, and yet interesting form. The demand I have had for separate copies of my lectures may moreover excuse, if not justify, their republication.

HIGH ELMS, DOWN, KENT,
   18*th March*, 1879.

CONTENTS.

LIST OF ILLUSTRATIONS.

PLATES.

SCIENTIFIC LECTURES.

FIG. 1.—*Lamium album.*

ON FLOWERS AND INSECTS.

LECTURE I.

THE flower of the Common White Deadnettle (*Lamium album*, Fig. 1) consists of a narrow tube, somewhat

FIG. 2.—Flower of *Lamium album.*

FIG. 3.—Section of ditto.

expanded at the upper end (Fig. 2), where the lower lobe of the corolla forms a platform, on each side of

which is a small projecting lobe (Fig. 3, *m*). The upper
portion of the corolla is an arched hood (Fig. 3, *co*),
under which lie four anthers (*a a*), in pairs, while
between them, and projecting somewhat downwards,
is the pointed pistil (*st*). At the lower part, the tube
contains honey, and above the honey is a row of hairs
almost closing the tube. Now, why has the flower this
peculiar form ? What regulates the length of the tube ?
What is the use of this arch ? What lessons do these
lobes teach us ? What advantage is the honey to the
flower ? Of what use is the fringe of hairs ? Why does
the stigma project beyond the anthers ? Why is the
corolla white, while the rest of the plant is green ?

Similar questions may of course be asked with reference to other flowers. Let us now see whether we can
throw any light upon them.

At the close of the last century, Conrad Sprengel published a valuable work on flowers, in which he pointed
out that the forms and colours, the scent, honey, and
general structure of flowers, have reference to the visits
of insects, which are of importance in transferring the
pollen from the stamens to the pistil. This admirable
work, however, did not attract the attention it deserved,
and remained almost unknown until Mr. Darwin devoted
himself to the subject. Our illustrious countryman was
the first clearly to perceive that the essential service
which insects perform to flowers, consists not only in
transferring the pollen from the stamens to the pistil,
but in transferring it from the stamens of one flower
to the pistil of another. Sprengel had indeed observed
in more than one instance that this was the case, but he
did not altogether appreciate the importance of the fact.

Mr. Darwin, however, has not only made it clear from theoretical considerations, but has also proved it, in a variety of cases, by actual experiment. More recently Fritz Müller has even shown that in some cases pollen, if placed on the stigma of the same flower, has no more effect than so much inorganic dust; while, and this is perhaps even more extraordinary, in others the pollen placed on the stigma of the same flower acted on it like a poison. This he observed in several species; the flowers faded and fell off, the pollen masses themselves, and the stigma in contact with them shrivelled up, turned brown, and decayed; while flowers on the same bunch, which were left unfertilized, retained their freshness.

The importance of this "cross-fertilization," as it may be called, in contradistinction to "self-fertilization," was first conclusively proved by Mr. Darwin in his remarkable memoir on Primula (*Linnean Journal*, 1862), and he has since illustrated the same rule by researches on Orchids, Linum, Lythrum, and a variety of other plants. The new impulse thus given to the study of flowers has been followed up in this country by Hooker, Ogle, Bennett, and other naturalists, and on the Continent by Axell, Delpino, Hildebrand, Kerner, F. Müller, and especially by Dr. H. Müller, who has published two excellent works on the subject, bringing together the observations of others, and adding to them an immense number of his own.

In by far the majority of cases, the relation between flowers and insects is one of mutual advantage. In some plants, however, as for instance in our Common Drosera, we find a very different state of things, and the plant catches and devours the insects.[1] The first observation on insect-eating flowers was made about the year 1768 by our countryman Ellis. He observed that in 'Dionæa, a North American plant, the leaves have a joint in the middle, and thus close over, kill, and actually digest any insect which may alight on them.

In our Common Sundew (*Drosera rotundifolia*, Fig. 4) the rounded leaves are covered with glutinous glandular

hairs or tentacles—on an average about 200 on a full-sized leaf. The glands are each surrounded by a drop of an exceedingly viscid solution, which, glittering in the sun, has given rise to the name of the plant. If any object be placed on the leaf, these glandular hairs slowly fold over it, but if it be inorganic they soon unfold again. On the other hand, if any small insect alights on the leaf it becomes entangled

FIG. 4.—*Drosera rotundifolia.*

in the glutinous secretion, the glands close over it, their secretion is increased, and they literally digest their prey. Mr. Frank Darwin has recently shown that plants supplied with insects grow more vigorously than those not so fed. It is very curious that while the glands are so sensitive that even an object weighing only $\frac{1}{78740}$th of a grain placed on them is sufficient to cause motion, yet they are "insensible to the weight and repeated blows of drops" of even heavy rain.

Drosera, however, is not our only English insect-

[1] See Darwin's *Insectivorous Plants.*

ivorous plant. In the genus Pinguicula, which frequents moist places, generally on mountains, the leaves are concave with incurved margins, and the upper surfaces are covered with two sets of glandular hairs. In this case the naturally incurved edges curve over still more if a fly or other insect be placed on the leaf.

Another case is that of Utricularia, an aquatic species, which bears a number of utricles or sacs, which have been supposed to act as floats. Branches, however, which bear no bladder float just as well as the others, and there seems no doubt that their real use is to capture small aquatic animals, which they do in considerable numbers. The bladders in fact are on the principle of an eel-trap, having an entrance closed with a flap which permits an easy entrance, but effectually prevents the unfortunate victim from getting out again.

I will only allude to one foreign case, that of the Sarracenia.[1] In this genus some of the leaves are in the form of a pitcher. They secrete a fluid, and are lined internally with hairs pointing downwards. Up the outside of the pitcher there is a line of honey glands which lure the insects to their destruction. Flies and other insects which fall into this pitcher cannot get out again, and are actually digested by the plant. Bees, however, are said to be scarcely ever caught.

Every one knows how important flowers are to insects; every one knows that bees, butterflies, &c., derive the main part of their nourishment from the honey or pollen of flowers, but comparatively few are aware, on the other hand, how much the flowers themselves are dependent on insects. Yet it has, I think, been clearly

[1] See Hooker, *British Association Journal*, 1874.

shown that if insects have been in some respects modified and adapted with a view to the acquirement of honey and pollen, flowers, on the other hand, owe their scent and honey, their form and colour, to the agency of insects. Thus the lines and bands by which so many flowers are ornamented have reference to the position of the honey; and it may be observed that these honey-guides are absent in night flowers, where they of course would not show, and would therefore be useless, as for

FIG. 5.—*Lychnis vespertina.*   FIG. 6.—*Geranium sylvaticum.*

instance in *Lychnis vespertina* (Fig. 5) or *Silene nutans.* Night flowers, moreover, are generally pale; for instance, *Lychnis vespertina* is white, while *Lychnis diurna,* which flowers by day, is red.

Indeed, it may be laid down as a general rule that those flowers which are not fertilized by insects, as for instance those of the Beech, Oak, and most other forest trees, are small in size, and do not possess either colour, scent, or honey.

Before proceeding further let me briefly mention the terms used in describing the different parts of a flower.

If we examine a common flower, such for instance as a Geranium (Fig. 6), we shall find that it consists, firstly, of an outer envelope or *calyx*, sometimes tubular, sometimes consisting of separate leaves called *sepals;* secondly, an inner envelope or *corolla*, which is generally more or less coloured, and which, like the calyx, is sometimes tubular, sometimes composed of separate

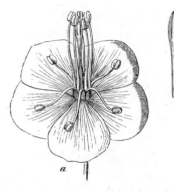
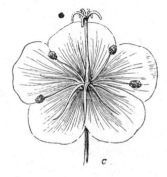

FIG. 7.—*Geranium pratense* (young flower). Five of the stamens are erect.

FIG. 8.—*Geranium pratense* (older flower). The stamens have retired, and the stigmas are expanded.

leaves called *petals;* thirdly, of one or more stamens, consisting of a stalk or *filament*, and a head or *anther*, in which the pollen is produced; and fourthly, a *pistil*, which is situated in the centre of the flower, and consists generally of three principal parts: one or more compartments at the base, each containing one or more seeds; the stalk or style; and the *stigma*, which in many familiar instances forms a small head at the top of the style or ovary, and to which the pollen must find its way in order to fertilize the flower.

But though the pistil is thus surrounded by a row of stamens there are comparatively few cases in which the pollen of the latter falls directly on the former. On the contrary this transference is in most cases effected in other ways—generally by means of the wind, of insects, or, in some cases, of birds. In the former case, however, by far the greater part of the pollen is wasted; and much more must therefore be produced than in those cases where the transference is effected by insects.

One advantage, of course, is the great economy of pollen. We have not much information on the subject, but it would seem, from the few observations that have been made, that half a dozen pollen grains are sufficient to fertilize a seed. But in plants in which the pollen is carried by the wind, the chances against any given grain reaching the pistil of another flower are immense. Consequently by far the greater part of the pollen is lost. Every one for instance must have observed the clouds of pollen produced by the Scotch Fir. In such flowers as the Pæony the pollen is carried by insects, and far less therefore is required; yet even here the quantity produced is still large; it has been estimated that each flower produces between 3,000,000 and 4,000,000 grains. The Dandelion is more specialized in this respect, and produces far less pollen; according to Mr. Hassall about 240,000 grains to each flower; while in *Geum urbanum*, according to Gærtner, only ten times more pollen is produced than is actually used in fertilization.

It might, however, be at first supposed that where stamens and pistil coexist in the same flower, the pollen from the one could easily fall on and fertilize the other. And in fact in some species this does occur; but as we have seen, it is a great advantage to a species that the flower should be fertilized by pollen from a different stock.   How then is self-fertilization prevented?

There are three principal modes.

Firstly, in many plants the stamens and pistil are in separate flowers, sometimes situated on different plants.

Secondly, even when the stamens and pistil are in the same flower, they are in many species not mature at the same time; this was first observed by Sprengel in *Epilobium angustifolium* (Fig. 13) as long ago as 1790; in some cases the stigma has matured before the anthers are ripe, while in other and more numerous cases the anthers have ripened and shed all their pollen before the stigma has come to maturity.

Thirdly, there are many species in which, though the anthers and stigma are contained in the same flower and are mature at the same time, they are so situated that the pollen can hardly reach the stigma of the same flower.

The transference of the pollen from one flower to another is, as already mentioned, effected principally either by the wind or by insects, though in some cases it is due to other agencies, as for instance, by birds, or by water.   For instance, in the curious *Vallisneria spiralis* the female flowers are situated on long stalks which are spirally twisted, and grow very rapidly, so that even if the level of the water alters, provided this be within certain limits, the flowers float on the surface.   The male flowers on the contrary are minute and sessile, but when mature they detach themselves from the plant, rise to the surface and float about freely like little boats among the female flowers.

Wind-fertilized flowers as a rule have no colour, emit no scent, produce no honey, and are regular in form. Colour, scent, and honey are the three characteristics by which insects are attracted to flowers.

Again, as a rule, wind-fertilized flowers produce much more pollen than those which are fertilized by insects. This is necessary, because it is obvious that the chances against any given pollen grain reaching the stigma are much greater in the one case than in the other. Every one, as already mentioned, has observed the showers of yellow pollen produced by the Scotch Fir.

Again, it is an advantage to wind-fertilized plants to flower early in the spring before the leaves are out, because the latter would catch much of the pollen and thus interfere with its access to the stigma. Again, in these plants the pollen is less adherent, so that it can easily be blown away by the wind, which would be a disadvantage in most plants which are fertilized by insects.

Again, such flowers generally have the stigma more or less branched or hairy, which evidently must tend to increase their chances of catching the pollen.

Moreover, as Mr. Darwin has observed (*Jour. Linn. Soc.*, vol. viii. p. 176), there does not appear to be a single instance of an irregular flower which is not fertilized by insects or birds.

The evidence derivable from the relations of bees and flowers is probably sufficient to satisfy most minds that bees are capable of distinguishing colours, but the fact had not been proved by any conclusive experiments. I

therefore tried the following. If you bring a bee to
some honey, she feeds quietly, goes back to the hive,
stores away her honey, and returns with or without
companions for another supply. Each visit occupies
about six minutes, so that there are about ten in an
hour, and about a hundred in a day. I may add that in
this respect the habits of wasps are very similar, and that
they appear to be quite as industrious as bees. Perhaps
I may give the record of a morning's work of one of
my wasps.[1] She came to the honey at a few minutes
after 4 in the morning, and to show how regularly
she worked I will give her record from 6.30 till 12.

She came at 6.29,	and returned at	6.32
Came again at 6.41	,,	6.44
,, 6.55	,,	7
,, 7.11	,,	7.15
,, 7.23	,,	7.26
,, 7.37	,,	7.42
,, 7.56	,,	8.3
,, 8.11	,,	8.14
,, 8.20	,,	8.24
,, 8.31	,,	8.34
,, 8.40	,,	8·42
,, 8.50	,,	8.52
,, 8.58	,,	9
,, 9.8	,,	9.11
,, 9.18	,,	9.22
,, 9.30	,,	9.32
,, 9.39	,,	9.40
,, 9.50	,,	9.54
,, 10.1	,,	10.5
,, 10.14	,,	10.17
,, 10.25	,,	10.28
,, 10.37	,,	10.40

[1] In her case the intervals were rather longer than usual.

Came again at 10.47, and returned at 10.51

,,	11	,,	11.6
,,	11.17	,,	11.20
,,	11.34	,,	11.37
,,.	11 50	,,	11.53
,,	12.5	,,	12.8

and so on till 6 in the evening; thus working twelve hours like a man, and performing more than a hundred journeys to and fro.[1] This, however, was in autumn; in summer they make overtime, and work on till late in the evening.

In order then to test the power of bees to appreciate colour, I placed some honey on a slip of glass, and put the glass on coloured paper. For instance, I put some honey in this manner on a piece of blue paper, and when a bee had made several journeys, and thus become accustomed to the blue colour, I placed some more honey in the same manner on orange paper about a foot away. Then during one of the absences of the bee I transposed the two colours, leaving the honey itself in the same place as before. The bee returned as usual to the place where she had been accustomed to find the honey; but though it was still there, she did not alight, but paused for a moment, and then dashed straight away to the blue

---

[1] The industry and **rapidity** with which bees work is very remarkable. They will visit from twenty to twenty-five flowers in a minute, which makes over 1,000 in an hour, or say 10,000 in a day. Mr. Darwin watched carefully certain flowers, and satisfied himself that each one was visited by bees at least thirty times in a day. The result is, that even where flowers are very numerous— as, for instance, on heathy plains and in clover fields—every one is visited during the day. Mr. Darwin carefully examined a large number of flowers in such cases, and found that every single one had been so visited.

paper. No one who saw my bee at that moment could have had the slightest doubt of her power of distinguishing blue from orange.

Again, having accustomed a bee to come to honey on blue paper, I ranged in a row other supplies of honey on glass slips placed over paper of other colours, yellow, orange, red, green, black, and white. Then I continually transposed the coloured paper, leaving the honey on the same spots; but the bee always flew to the blue paper, wherever it might be. Bees appear fortunately to prefer the same colours as we do. On the contrary, flowers of a livid, yellow, or fleshy colour are most attractive to flies; and moreover while bees are attracted by odours which are also agreeable to us, flies, as might naturally be expected from the habits of their larvæ, prefer some which to us seem anything but pleasant.

Among other obvious evidences that the beauty of flowers is useful in consequence of its attracting insects, we may adduce those cases in which the transference of the pollen is effected in different manners in nearly allied plants, sometimes even in the same genus.

Thus, as Dr. H. Müller has pointed out, *Malva sylvestris* (Fig. 9) and *Malva rotundifolia* (Fig. 10), which grow in the same localities, and therefore must come into competition, are nevertheless nearly equally common.

In *Malva sylvestris*, however (Fig. 11), where the branches of the stigma are so arranged that the plant cannot fertilize itself, the petals are large and conspicuous, so that the plant is visited by numerous insects; while in *Malva rotundifolia* the flowers of which are comparatively small and rarely visited by insects, the

branches of the stigma are elongated, and twine themselves (Fig. 12) among the stamens, so that the flower
readily fertilizes itself.

FIG. 9.—*Malva sylvestris.*   FIG. 10.—*Malva rotundifolia.*

Another interesting case is afforded by the genus
Epilobium. *Epilobium angustifolium* has large purplish
flowers in conspicuous heads (Fig. 13), and is much
frequented by insects; while *E. parviflorum* (Fig. 14)

FIG. 11.—Stamens and stigmas of   FIG. 12.—Ditto of *Malva rotundifolia.*
       Malva sylvestris.

has small solitary flowers and is seldom visited by
insects. Now in the former species their visits are
necessary, because the stamens ripen and shed their
pollen before the pistil, so that the flower is con-

sequently incapable of fertilizing itself. In *E. parvi-florum*, on the contrary, the stamens and pistil come to maturity at the same time.

FIG. 13.—*Epilobium angustifolium.*   FIG. 14.—*Epilobium parviflorum.*

Let us take another case—that of certain Geraniums. In *G. pratense* all the stamens open, shed their pollen, and wither away before the pistil comes to maturity. The flower cannot therefore fertilize itself, and depends entirely on the visits of insects for the transference of the pollen. In *G. pyrenaicum*, where the flower is not quite so large, all the stamens ripen before the stigma, but the interval is shorter, and the stigma is mature before all the anthers have shed their pollen. It is therefore not absolutely dependent on insects. In *G. molle*, which has a still smaller flower, five of the stamens come to maturity before the stigma, but the last five ripen simultaneously with it. Lastly, in *G. pusillum*, which is least of all, the stigma ripens even before the stamens. Thus, then, we have a series more or less dependent on insects, from *G. pratense* to which they are necessary, to *G. pusillum*, which is quite independent of them; while the size of the corolla increases with the dependence on insects.

In those species in which self-fertilization is prevented by the circumstance that the stamens and pistil do not come to maturity at the same time, the stamens generally ripen first.

The advantage of this is probably connected with the visits of bees. In those flowers which grow in bunches the lower ones generally open first. Consequently in any given spike the flowers are at first all male ; subsequently the lower ones, being the older, have arrived at the female stage while the upper ones are still male. Now it is the habit of bees to begin with the lower flowers of a spike and work upwards. A bee, therefore, which has already dusted herself with pollen from another flower, first comes in contact with the female flowers, and dusts them with pollen, after which she receives a fresh supply from the upper male flowers, with which she flies to another plant.

There are, however, some few species in which the pistil ripens before the stamens. One is our common *Scrophularia nodosa*. Now why is this ? Mr. Wilson has given us the answer. *S. nodosa* is one of our few flowers specially visited by wasps ; the honey being not pleasing to bees. Wasps, however, unlike bees, generally begin with the upper flowers and pass downwards, and consequently in wasp flowers it is an advantage that the pistil should ripen before the stamens. But though the stamens generally ripen before the pistil, the reverse sometimes occurs. Of this a very interesting case is that of the genus Aristolochia. The flower is a long tube, with a narrow opening closed by stiff hairs which point backwards, so that it much resembles an ordinary eel-trap. Small flies enter the tube in search of honey, but from the direction of the hairs it is impossible for them to return. Thus they are imprisoned in the flower until the stamens have ripened and shed their pollen, by which the flies get thoroughly dusted. Then the hairs of the tube shrivel up, thus releasing the prisoners, which carry the pollen to another flower.

Again, in our common Arums—the Lords and Ladies of village children—the well-known green leaf incloses a central pillar ; near the base of which are arranged a number of stigmas (*st* in the accompanying figure), and above them several rows of anthers (*a*). It might be supposed therefore that the pollen from the anthers would fall on and fertilize the stigmas. This, however, is not what occurs. In fact the stigmas come to maturity first, and have lost the possibility of fertilization before the pollen is ripe. The pollen must therefore be brought by insects, and this is effected by small flies, which enter the leaf, either for the sake of honey or of shelter, and which, moreover, when they have once

FIG. 15. — Diagrammatic section of Arum.   *h*, hairs: *a*, anthers ;   *st*, stigmas.

entered the tube, are imprisoned by the fringe of hairs (*h*). When the anthers ripen, the pollen falls on to the flies, which in their efforts to escape get thoroughly dusted with it. Then the fringe of hairs withers, and the flies, thus set free, soon come out, and ere long carry the pollen to another plant.

Now let us return to our White Deadnettle and

C

see how far we can answer the questions which I began by asking.

In the first place, the honey attracts insects. If there were no honey, they would have no object in visiting the flower. The bright colour is useful in rendering the flower conspicuous. The platform serves as an alighting stage for bees. The length of the tube has reference to that of their proboscis, and prevents the smaller species from obtaining access to the honey, which would be injurious to the flower, as it would remove the source of attraction for the bees, without effecting the object in view. The upper arch of the flower protects the stamens and pistil, and also presses them firmly against the back of the bee. So that, when the bee alights on the stage and pushes its proboscis down to the honey, its back comes into contact with them. The row of small hairs at the bottom of the tube prevents small insects from creeping down the tube and stealing the honey. Lastly, the small processes on each side of the lower lip are the rudimentary representatives of parts, formerly more largely developed, but which, having become useless, have almost disappeared.

In the Deadnettle, it would appear that the pistil matures as early as the stamens, and that cross-fertilization is attained by the relative position of the stigma, which, as will be seen in the figure, hangs down below the stamens; so that a bee, bearing pollen on its back from a previous visit to another flower, would touch the pistil and transfer to it some of the pollen, before coming in contact with the stamens. In other species belonging to the same great group (Labiatæ) as Lamium, the same object is secured by the fact that the stamens

come to maturity before the pistil; they shed their
pollen, and shrivel up before the stigma is mature.

Fig. 16 represents a young flower of *Salvia officinalis*,
in which the stamens (*a a*) are mature, but not the pistil
(*p*), which, moreover, from its position, is untouched

Fig. 16.

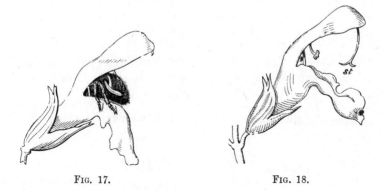

Fig. 17.   Fig. 18.

Fig. 16.—*Salvia officinalis.* Section of a young flower.
Fig. 17.—Ditto, visited by a bee.
Fig. 18.—Ditto, older flower.

by bees visiting the flower; as shown in Fig. 17. The
anthers, as they shed their pollen, gradually shrivel up;
while, on the other hand, the pistil increases in length
and curves downwards, until it assumes the position
shown in Fig. 18, *st*, where, as is evident, it must come

in contact with any bee visiting the flower, and would touch just that spot of the back on which pollen would be deposited by a younger flower. In this manner cross-fertilization is effectually secured.

There are, however, several other curious points in which *S. officinalis* differs greatly from the species last described.

The general form of the flower, indeed, is very similar. We find again that, as generally in the Labiates, the corolla has the lower lip adapted as an alighting board for insects, while the arched upper lip covers and protects the stamens and pistils.

The arrangement and structure of the stamens is, however, very peculiar and interesting. As in Lamium, they are four in number, but one pair is quite rudimentary (Fig. 16). In the other (*a a*) the two anthers, instead of being attached close together at the summit of the filament, are separated by a long movable rod, or connective (Figs. 19, 20, *m*), so that they can play freely on the stalk of the stamen. In a natural position, this connective is upright, so that the one anther is situated (Fig. 16) in the neck of the tube, the other under the arched hood. The lower anther, moreover, is more or less rudimentary. Now when a bee comes to suck the honey, it pushes the lower anther out of the way with its head ; the result of which is that the connective swings round, and the upper fertile anther comes down on to the back of the bee (Figs. 17 and 20), and dusts it with pollen, just at the place where, in an older flower (Fig. 18) it would be touched by the stigma, *st.*

At first sight, it may seem an objection to this view that some species—as, for instance, the Common

Antirrhinum, which, according to the above given tests ought to be fertilized by insects, is entirely closed. A little consideration, however, will suggest the reply. The Antirrhinum is especially adapted for fertilization by humble bees. The stamens and pistil are so arranged

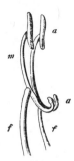

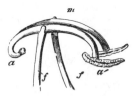

FIG. 19.—Stamens in their natural position.

FIG. 20.—Stamens when moved by a Bee.

that smaller species would not effect the object. It is therefore an advantage that they should be excluded, and in fact they are not strong enough to move the spring. The Antirrhinum is, so to speak, a closed box, of which the humble bees alone possess the key.

The Common Heath (*Erica tetralix*) offers us a very ingenious arrangement. The flower is in the form of an inverted bell. The pistil represents the clapper, and projects a little beyond the mouth of the bell. The stamens are eight in number, and form a circle round it, the anthers being united by their sides into a continuous ring. Each anther has a lateral hole, but as long as they touch one another, the pollen cannot drop out. Each also sends out a long process, so that the ring of anthers is surrounded by a row of spokes. Now when a bee comes to suck the honey, it first touches the end of the pistil, on which it could hardly fail to deposit some pollen, had it previously visited another plant. It would then press its proboscis up the bell, in doing which it would pass between two of the spokes, and pressing them apart, would dislocate the ring of anthers : a shower of pollen would thus fall upon the open cells on to the head of the bee.

FIG. 21.—Wild Chervil (*Chœro-phyllum sylvestre*).

In many cases the effect of the colouring and scent is greatly enhanced by the association of several flowers in one bunch, or raceme ; as for instance in the wild hyacinth, the lilac, and other familiar species. In the great family of Umbellifera, this arrangement is still further taken advantage of, as in the Common Wild Chervil (*Chœrophyllum sylvestre*, Fig. 21).

In this group the honey is not, as in the flowers just described, situated at the bottom of a tube, but lies exposed, and is therefore accessible to a great variety of small insects. The union of the florets into a head, moreover, not only renders them more conspicuous, but also enables the insects to visit a greater number of flowers in a given time.

It might at first be supposed that in such small flowers as these self-fertilization would be almost unavoidable. In most cases, however, the stamens ripen before the stigmas.

The position of the honey on the surface of a more or

less flat disk renders it much more accessible than in those cases in which it is situated at the end of a more or less long tube. That of the Deadnettle, for instance, is only accessible to certain humble bees; while H. Müller has recorded no less than seventy-three species of insects as visiting the Common Chervil, and some plants are frequented by even a larger number.

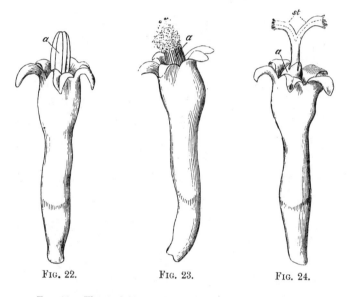

FIG. 22.   FIG. 23.   FIG. 24.

FIG. 22.—Floret of *Chrysanthemum parthenium*, just opened.
FIG. 23.—Ditto, somewhat more advanced.
FIG. 24.—Ditto, with the stigmas expanded.

In the Composites, to which the Common Daisy and the Dandelion belong, the association of flowers is carried so far, that a whole group of florets is ordinarily spoken of as one flower. Let us take, for instance, the Common Feverfew, or large white Daisy (*Chrysanthemum parthenium*, Figs. 22—24). Each head consists of an outer row of female florets, in

which the tubular corolla terminates on its outer side in
a white leaf-ovary, which serves to make the flower more
conspicuous, and thus to attract insects. The central
florets are tubular, and make up the central yellow part
of the flower-head. Each of these florets contains a
circle of stamens, the upper portions of which are united
at their edges and at the top (Fig. 22), so as to form a
tube, within which is the pistil. The anthers open
inwards, so as to shed the pollen into this box, the lower
part of which is formed by the stigma, or upper part of
the pistil. As the latter elongates, it presses the pollen
against the upper part of the box, which at length is forced
open, and the pollen is pushed out (Fig. 23). Any insect
then alighting on the flower would carry off some of the
pollen adhering to its under side. The upper part of
the pistil terminates in two branches (Fig. 24, *st*), each of
which bears a little brush of hairs. These hairs serve to
brush the pollen out of the tube ; while in the tube the
two branches are pressed close together, but at a later
stage they separate, and thus expose the stigmatic surfaces (Fig. 23), on which an insect, coming from a
younger flower, could hardly fail to deposit some pollen.
The two stigmas in the ray florets of Parthenium have
no brush of hairs ; and they would be of no use, as these
flowers have no stamens.

The Leguminosæ, or Pea-tribe, present a number of
beautiful contrivances. Let us take a common little
Lotus corniculatus (Fig. 25). The petals are five in
number ; the upper one stands upright, and is known as
the standard (Fig. 26, *std*) ; the two lateral ones present
a slight resemblance to wings (Figs. 26, 27, *w*), while
the two lower ones are united along their edges so

as to form a sort of boat, whence they are known
as the "keel" (Figs. 27, 28, k). The stamens, with
one exception, are united at
their bases, thus forming a tube
(Figs. 29, 30, t), surrounding
the pistil, which projects beyond them into a triangular
space at the end of the keel.
Into this space the pollen is
shed (Fig. 30, p^o). It must
also be observed that each of
the wings has a projection (c)
which locks into a corresponding depression of the keel, so
that if the wings are depressed
they carry the keel with them.

FIG. 25.—*Lotus corniculatus.*

Now when an insect alights on the flower, its weight
depresses the wings, and as they again carry with them
the keel, the latter slips over the column of stamens,
thus forcing some of the pollen out at the end of the
keel and against the breast of the insect. As soon as
the insect leaves the flower, this resumes its natural
position, and the pollen is again snugly protected. The
arrangement in the Sweet Pea is very similar, and if
the wings are seized by the fingers, and pressed down,
this out-pumping of the pollen may be easily effected,
and the mechanism will then be more clearly understood.

It will be observed (Fig. 30) that one stamen is separated from the rest. The advantage of this is that it
leaves a space through which the proboscis of the bee
can reach the honey, which is situated inside the tube
formed by the united stamens. In those Leguminosæ

which have no honey, the stamens are all united together. Such flowers are, nevertheless, in spite of the

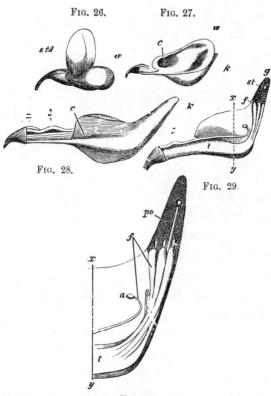

FIG. 26.   FIG. 27.

FIG. 28.

FIG. 29.

FIG. 30.

FIG. 26.—Flower of *Lotus corniculatus*, seen from the side and in front.
FIG. 27.—Ditto, after removal of the standard.
FIG. 28.—Ditto, after removal of the standard and wings.
FIG. 29.—Ditto, after removal of one side of the keel.
FIG. 30.—Terminal portion of Fig. 29 more magnified.
   e, entrance to the honey ; *a*, the free stamen ; *c*, the place where the
      wings lock with the keel ; *f'*, expanded ends of stamens ; *f*, fila-
      ments of stamens ; *g*, tip of keel ; *po*, pollen ; *st*, stigma.

absence of honey, visited by insects for the sake of the
pollen.

In other Leguminosæ, as for instance in the Furze

(*Ulex europæus*), and the Broom (*Sarothamnus scoparius*), the flower is in a state of tension, but the different parts are, as it were, locked together. The action of the bee, however, puts an end to this; the flower explodes, and thus dusts the bee with pollen.

It would, however, take too long to refer to the various interesting arrangements by which cross-fertilization is secured in this great order of plants.

It is impossible not to be struck by the marvellous variety of contrivances found among flowers, and the light thus thrown upon them, by the consideration of their relations to insects; but I must now call your attention to certain very curious cases, in which the same species has two or more kinds of flowers. Probably in all plants the flowers differ somewhat in size, and I have already mentioned (*ante*, p. 13) some species in which these differences have given rise to two distinct classes of flowers, one large, and much visited by insects, the other small, and comparatively neglected. In other species, as, for instance, some of the Violets, these differences are carried much further. The smaller flowers have no smell or honey, the corolla is rudimentary, and, in fact, an ordinary observer would not recognize them as flowers at all. Such "cleistogamic" flowers, as they have been termed by Dr. Kuhn, are already known to exist in about fifty genera. Their object probably is to secure, with as little expenditure as possible, the continuance of the species, in cases when, from unfavourable weather or other causes, insects are absent; and under such circumstances, as scent, honey, and colour are of no use, it is an advantage to the plant to be spared from the effort of their production.

As the type of another class of cases in which two
kinds of flowers are produced by the same species (though
not on the same stock) we may take our common Cow-
slips and Primroses.   If you examine a number of them,
you will find that they fall into two distinct series.   In
some of the flowers, the pistil is as long as the tube, and
the button-shaped stigma (Fig. 31, *st*) is situated at the
mouth of the flower; the stamens (*a a*) being half-way
down the tube: while in the other set, on the contrary,
the anthers are at the mouth of the flower, and the

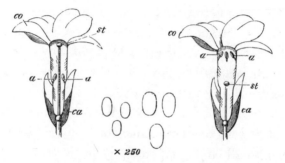

FIG. 31.—Primula (long-styled form).   FIG. 32.—Primula (short-styled form).

stigma half-way down.   The existence of these two
kinds of flowers had long been known, but it remained
unexplained until Mr. Darwin devoted his attention to
the subject.   Now that he has furnished us with the
clue, the case is clear enough.

An insect visiting a plant of the short-styled form
would dust its proboscis at a certain distance from the
extremity (Fig. 32, *a*), which, when the insect passed to
a long-styled flower, would come just opposite to the
pistil (Fig. 31, *st*).   At the same time, the stamens of
this second form (Fig. 31, *a*) would dust the proboscis at

a point considerably nearer to the extremity, which in
its turn would correspond to the position of the stigma
in the first form (Fig. 32, *st*).   The two kinds of flowers
never grow together on the same stock, and the two
kinds of plants generally grow together in nearly equal
proportions.   Owing to this arrangement, therefore, insects can hardly fail to fertilize each flower with pollen
from a different stock.

The two forms differ also in some other respects.   In
the long-styled form, the stigma (*st*) is globular and
rough, while that of the short-styled is smoother, and
somewhat depressed.   These differences, however, are
not sufficiently conspicuous to be shown in the figure.
Again, the pollen of the long-styled form is considerably
smaller than the other, a difference the importance of
which is obvious, for each has to give rise to a tube
which penetrates the whole length of the style, from the
stigma to the base of the flower ; and the one has therefore to produce a tube nearly twice as long as that of
the other.   The careful experiments made by Mr. Darwin
have shown that, to obtain the largest quantity of seed,
the flowers must be fertilized by pollen from the other
form.   Nay, in some cases, the flowers produce more seed,
if fertilized by pollen from another species, than by that
from the other form of their own.

This curious difference in the Primrose and Cowslip,
between flowers of the same species, which Mr. Darwin
has proposed to call Dimorphism, is found in most
species of the genus *Primula*, but not in all.

The Cowslip and Primrose resemble one another in
many respects, but the honey they secrete must be very
different, for while the Cowslip is habitually visited

during the day by humble bees, this is not the case with
the Primrose, which, in Mr. Darwin's opinion, is fertilized
almost exclusively by moths.

The genus Lythrum (Fig. 33) affords a still more
complex case, for here we have three sets of flowers.

The stamens are in two groups;
in some plants, the pistil projects
beyond them; in the second form
it is shorter than any of the stamens, and in the third it is intermediate in length, so that the
stigma lies between the two sets
of anthers. These three positions
appear to correspond respectively
to the head, thorax, and abdomen
of the bee.

Although flowers present us
with these beautiful and complex
contrivances, whereby the transfer

FIG. 33.—*Lythrum salicaria.*

of pollen from flower to flower is provided for, and
waste is prevented, yet they appear to be imperfect,
or at least not yet perfect in their adaptations. Many
small insects obtain access to flowers and rob them
of their contents. *Malva rotundifolia* can be, and
often is, sucked by bees from the outside, in which
case the flower derives no advantage from the visit
of the insect. In *Medicago sativa*, also, insects can
suck the honey without effecting fertilization, and the
same flower continues to secrete honey after fertilization has taken place, and when, apparently, it can
no longer be of any use. Fritz Müller has observed
that, though *Posqueria fragrans* is exclusively fer-

tilized by night-flying insects, many of the flowers open
in the day, and consequently remain sterile. It is
of course possible that these cases may be explained
away ; nevertheless, as both insects and flowers are continually altering in their structure, and in their geographical distribution, we should naturally expect to
find such instances. Water continually tends to find its
own level ; animals and plants as constantly tend to adapt
themselves to their conditions. For it is obvious that
any blossom which differed from the form and size best
adapted to secure the due transference of the pollen
would be less likely to be fertilized than others ; while
on the other hand, those richest in honey, sweetest, and
most conspicuous, would most surely attract the attention and secure the visits of insects ; and thus, just as
our gardeners, by selecting seed from the most beautiful varieties, have done so much to adorn our gar-
dens, so have insects, by fertilizing the largest and
most brilliant flowers, contributed unconsciously, but
not less effectually, to the beauty of our woods and
fields.[1]

[1] I have treated the subject of this lecture at greater length in a
little book on Flowers and Insects, forming one of the "Nature
Series."

ON PLANTS AND INSECTS.

LECTURE II.

In the last lecture I endeavoured to show in a variety of cases how beautifully flowers are constructed, so as to secure their fertilization by insects. Neither plants nor insects would be what they are, but for the influence which each has exercised on the other. Some plants, indeed, are altogether dependent on insects for their very existence. We know now, for instance, that certain plants produce no seeds at all, unless visited by insects. Thus, in some of our colonies, the common Red Clover sets no seeds, on account of the absence of humble bees; for the proboscis of the hive bee is not long enough to effect the object. According to Mr. Belt, the same is the case, and for the same reason, in Nicaragua, with the scarlet-runner. But even in those instances in which it is not absolutely necessary, it is an advantage that the flowers should be fertilized by pollen brought from a different stock, and with this object in view, insects are tempted to visit flowers for the sake of the honey and pollen; while the colours and scents are useful in making the flowers more easy to find.

Fortunately for us, bees like the same odours as we do; and as the great majority of flowers are adapted for bees,

they are consequently sweet; but it might have been
otherwise, for flies prefer unpleasant smells, such as those
of decaying meat and other animal substances on which
they live as larvæ, and some flowers, consequently,
which are fertilized by them, are characterized by very
evil odours. Colours also are affected in the same
manner, for while bee-flowers (if I may coin such an
expression) have generally bright, clear colours, fly-
flowers are usually reddish or yellowish brown

The real use of honey now seems so obvious that it
is curious to see the various theories which were once
entertained on the subject. Patrick Blair thought that
the honey absorbed the pollen, and then fertilized the
ovary ; Pontedera that it kept the ovary in a moist
condition. Linnæus confessed his inability to solve the
question. Other botanists considered that it was useless
material thrown off in the process of growth. Krünitz
thought he observed that in meadows much visited by
bees the plants were more healthy, but the inference he
drew was, that the honey, unless removed, was very injurious, and that the bees were of use in carrying it off.

Kurr observed that the formation of honey in flowers
is intimately associated with the maturity of the stamens
and pistil. He lays it down, as a general rule, that it
very seldom commences before the opening of the anthers, is generally most copious during their maturity,
and ceases so soon as the stamens begin to wither and
the development of the fruit commences. Rothe's
observations also led him to a similar conclusion, and
yet neither of these botanists perceived the intimate
association which exists between the presence of honey

D

and the period at which the visits of insects are of
importance to the plant.   Sprengel was the first to
point out the real office of honey, but his views were
far from meeting with general assent, and, even as
lately as 1833, were altogether rejected by Kurr, who
came to the conclusion that the secretion of honey is
the result of developmental energy, which afterwards
concentrates itself on the ovary.

No doubt, however, seems any longer to exist that
Sprengel's view is right; and that the true function of
honey is to attract insects, and thus to secure cross-
fertilization.   Thus, most of the Rosaceæ are fertilized
by insects, and possess nectaries; but, as Delpino has
pointed out, the genus Poterium is anemophilous, or
wind-fertilized, and possesses no honey.   So also the
Maples are almost all fertilized by insects, and produce
honey ; but *Acer negundo* is anemophilous, and honey-
less.   Again, among the Polygonaceæ, some species are
insect-fertilized and melliferous, while, on the other hand,
certain genera, Rumex and Oxyria, have no honey, and
are fertilized by the wind.   At first sight it might
appear an objection to this view,—and one reason
perhaps why the earlier botanists missed the true explanation may have been the fact,—that some plants
secrete honey on other parts than the flowers.   Belt
and Delpino have, I think, suggested the true function
of these extra-floral nectaries.[1]   The former of these
excellent observers describes a South American species
of Acacia : this tree, if unprotected, is apt to be stripped

[1] I by no means, however, wish to suggest that we as yet fully
understand the facts.   For instance, the use of the nectary at the
base of the leaf of the fern is still quite unexplained.

of the leaves by a leaf-cutting ant, which uses them, not directly for food, but, according to Mr. Belt, to grow mushrooms on. The Acacia, however, bears hollow thorns, while each leaflet produces honey in a crater-formed gland at the base, and a small, sweet, pear-shaped body at the tip. In consequence, it is inhabited by myriads of a small ant, which nests in the hollow thorns, and thus finds meat, drink, and lodging all provided for it. These ants are continually roaming over the plant, and constitute a most efficient body-guard, not only driving off the leaf-cutting ants, but, in Belt's opinion, rendering the leaves less liable to be eaten by herbivorous mammalia. Delpino mentions that on one occasion he was gathering a flower of *Clerodendron fragrans*, when he was suddenly attacked by a whole army of small ants.

I am not aware that any of our English plants are protected in this manner from browsing quadrupeds, but not the less do our ants perform for them a very similar function, by keeping down the number of small insects, which would otherwise rob them of their sap and strip them of their leaves.

Forel watched, from this point of view, a nest of *Formica pratensis.* He found that the ants brought in dead insects, small caterpillars, grasshoppers, cercopis, &c., at the rate of about twenty-eight a minute, or more than one thousand six hundred in an hour. When it is considered that the ants work not only all day, but in warm weather often all night too, it is easy to see how important a function they fulfil in keeping down the number of small insects.

Some of the most mischievous insects, indeed—certain

species, for instance, of aphis and coccus—have turned the tables on the plants, and converted ants from enemies into friends, by themselves developing nectaries, and secreting honey, which the ants love. We have all seen the little brown garden ant, for instance, assiduously running up the stems of plants, to milk their curious little cattle. In this manner, not only do the aphides and cocci secure immunity from the attacks of the ants, but even turn them from foes into friends. They are subject to the attacks of a species of ichneumon, which lays its eggs in them, and Delpino has seen ants watching over the cocci with truly maternal vigilance, and driving off the ichneumons whenever- they attempted to approach.

But though ants are in some respects very useful to plants, they are not wanted in the flowers. The great object is to secure cross-fertilization; but for this purpose winged insects are almost necessary, because they fly readily from one plant to another, and generally, as already mentioned, confine themselves for a certain time to the same species. Creeping insects, on the other hand, naturally would pass from each floret to the next; and, as Mr. Darwin has shown in his last work, it is of little use to bring pollen from a different flower of the same stock; it must be from a different plant altogether. Moreover, creeping insects, in quitting a plant, would generally go up another close by, without any regard to species. Hence, even to small flowers (such as many Cruciferæ, Compositæ, Saxifrages, &c.), which, as far as size is concerned, might well be fertilized by ants, the visits of flying insects are much more advantageous.

Moreover, if larger flowers were visited by ants, not only would these deprive the flowers of their honey, without fulfilling any useful function in return, but they would probably prevent the really useful visits of bees. If you touch an ant with a needle or a bristle, she is almost sure to seize it in her jaws; and if bees, when visiting any particular species, were liable to have the delicate tip of their proboscis seized on by the horny jaws of an ant, we may be sure that such a plant would soon be deserted.

On the other hand, we know how fond ants are of honey, and how zealously and unremittingly they search for food. How is it, then, that they do not anticipate the bees, and secure the honey for themselves? Kerner has recently published a most interesting memoir on this subject, and has pointed out a number of in-genious contrivances by which flowers protect them selves from the unwelcome visits of such intruders. The most frequent are the interposition of *chevaux de frise*, which ants cannot penetrate, glutinous parts which they cannot traverse, slippery slopes which they cannot climb, or barriers which close the way.

Firstly, then, as regards *chevaux de frise*. In some respects these are the most effectual protection, since they exclude not only creeping insects, but also other creatures, such as slugs. With this object, it will be observed that the hairs which cover the stalks of so many herbs usually point downwards. A good example of this is afforded, for instance, by a plant, *Knautia dip-sacifolia* (Fig. 34), allied to our Common Blue Scabious. The heads of the Common Carline (*Carlina vulgaris*) (Fig. 36), again, present a sort of thicket, which must

offer an almost impenetrable barrier to ants. Some
species of plants are quite smooth, excepting just below
the flowers. The common but beautiful Cornflower
(*Centaurea cyanus*) is quite smooth, but the involucres
forming the flower-head are bordered with recurved
teeth. In this case, neither the stem nor the leaves
show a trace of such prickles.

The same consideration throws light on the large
number of plants which are more or less glutinous, a
condition generally produced, as, for instance, in the

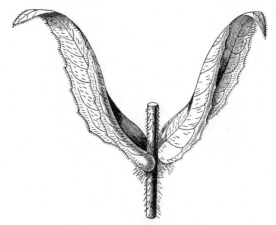

FIG. 34.—*Knautia dipsacifolia.*

flowers of the Gooseberry and of *Linnæa borealis* (Fig.
35), by the presence of glandular hairs. Kerner has
called attention to a very interesting illustration afforded
by *Polygonum amphibium*. In this species the stigma
projects about one-fifth of an inch above the flower, so
that if ants could obtain access, they would steal the
honey without fertilizing the flower; a flying insect,
on the contrary, alighting on the flower, could scarcely
fail to touch the stigma.

The beautiful rosy flowers of this species are rich in nectar : the stamens are short ; the pistil, on the contrary, projects considerably above the corolla. The nectar is not protected by any special arrangement of the flower itself, and is accessible even to very small insects. The stamens ripen before the pistil, and any flying insect, however small, coming from above, would assist in cross-fertilization. Creeping insects, on the contrary, which in most cases would enter from below, would rob the honey without benefiting the plant. *P. amphibium*, as its name denotes, grows

Fig. 35.—*Linnœa.*   Fig. 36.—*Carlina.*

sometimes in water, sometimes on land. So long, of course, as it grows in water, it is thoroughly protected, and the stem is smooth ; while, on the other hand, those specimens which live on land throw out certain hairs which terminate in sticky glands, and thus prevent small insects from creeping up to the flowers. In this case, therefore, the plant is not sticky, except just when this condition is useful. All these viscous plants, as far as I know, have upright or horizontal flowers.

On the other hand, where the same object is effected by slippery surfaces, the flowers are often pendulous ;

creeping creatures being thus kept out of them, just as
the pendulous nests of the weaver-bird are a protection
from snakes and other enemies.   As instances of this
kind, I may mention the Common Snowdrop, and the
Cyclamen.

Many flowers close their petals during rain, and this
is obviously an advantage, since it prevents the honey
and pollen from being spoilt or washed away.   I have
elsewhere suggested that the so-called "sleep" of flowers
has reference to the habits of insects, on the ground
that flowers which are fertilized by night-flying insects
would derive no advantage from being open in the day;
while, on the other hand, those which are fertilized by
bees would gain nothing by being open at night.   I
confess that I suggested this with much diffidence, but it
may now, I think, be regarded as well established.

Silene nutans (Fig. 37), the Nottingham Catchfly, is a
very instructive species from this point of view, and

FIG. 37.—*Silene nutans.*

indeed illustrates a number of
interesting points in the relations
between plants and insects.   Its
life history has recently been well
described by Kerner.   The upper
part of the flowering stem is
viscid; from which it has derived
its English name, the Nottingham
Catchfly.   This prevents the access
of ants and other small creeping insects.   Each flower
lasts three days, or rather three nights.   The stamens
are ten in number, arranged in two sets, the one set
standing in front of the sepals, the other in front

of the petals. Like other night flowers, it is white, and opens towards evening, when it also becomes extremely fragrant. The first evening, towards dusk, the five stamens in front of the sepals grow very rapidly for about two hours, so that they emerge from the flower; the pollen ripens, and is exposed by the bursting of the anther. So the flower remains through the night, very attractive to, and much visited by, moths. Towards three in the morning the scent ceases, the anthers begin to shrivel up or drop off, the filaments turn themselves outwards, so as to be out of the way, while the petals, on the contrary, begin to roll themselves up, so that by daylight they close the aperture of the flower, and present only their brownish-green undersides to view; which, moreover, are thrown into numerous wrinkles. Thus, by the morning's light, the flower has all the appearance of being faded. It has no smell, and the honey is covered over by the petals. So it remains all day. Towards evening, however, everything is changed. The petals unfold themselves; by eight o'clock the flower is as fragrant as before, the second set of stamens have rapidly grown, their anthers are open, and the pollen again exposed. By morning the flower is again "asleep," the anthers are shrivelled, the scent has ceased, and the petals rolled up as before. The third evening, again the same process occurs, but this time it is the pistil which grows: the long spiral stigmas on the third evening take the position which on the previous two had been occupied by the anthers, and can hardly fail to be dusted by moths with pollen brought from another flower.

An objection to the view that the sleep of flowers is regulated by the visits of insects, might be derived from the cases of those flowers which close early in the day, the well-known *Tragopogon pratense,* or "John Go-to-bed at Noon," for instance ; still more, such species as *Lapsana communis,* or *Crepis pulchra,* which open before six and close again before ten in the morning. Bees, however, are early risers, and some species, as for instance some of the Halicti, cease visiting flowers before the heat of the day commences, while ants come out later, when the dew is off; so that it might be an advantage to a flower which was quite unprotected, to open early for the bees, and close again before the ants were out (see *ante,* p. 36), thus preserving its honey exclusively for bees.

So much for the first part of my subject. I must now pass to the second—the action of plants upon insects. It would here, perhaps, be most natural to discuss the modifications which have been produced in insects by the search after honey and pollen ; especially the gradual lengthening of the proboscis in butterflies, moths, and bees, to enable them to suck the honey, and the adaptation of the legs of bees, to enable them to carry off the more or less dry and dusty pollen. Having, however, already said so much about flowers and insects, it will be better for me to take other illustrations, and fortunately there is no lack or difficulty.

Many of the cases in which certain insects escape danger by their similarity to plants are well known ; the leaf insect and the walking-stick insect are familiar and most remarkable cases. The larvæ of insects afford, also, many interesting examples, and, in other respects, teach us, indeed, many instructive lessons. It would be a great mistake to regard them as merely preparatory stages in the development of the perfect insect. They are much more than this, for external circumstances act on the larvæ, as well as on the perfect insect : both, therefore, are liable to adaptation.   In fact, the modifications which insect larvæ undergo may be divided into two kinds— developmental, or those which tend to approximation to the mature form ; and adaptational or adaptive ; those which tend to suit them to their own mode of life.

It is a remarkable fact, that the forms of larvæ do not depend on that of the mature insect.   In many cases, for instance, very similar larvæ produce extremely dissimilar insects.   In other cases, similar, or comparatively similar, perfect insects have very dissimilar larvæ.   Indeed, a classification of insects founded on larvæ would be quite different from that founded on the perfect insects. The *Hymenoptera*, for instance, which, so far as the perfect insects are concerned, form a very homogeneous group, would be divided into two—or rather one portion of them, namely, the saw-flies, would be united to the butterflies and moths.   Now, why do the larvæ of saw-flies differ from those of other *Hymenoptera*, and re-semble those of butterflies and moths ?   It is because their habits differ from those of other *Hymenoptera*, and they feed on leaves, like ordinary caterpillars.

In some cases the form changes considerably during the larval state.   From this point of view, the trans-formations of the genus Sitaris, which has been carefully investigated by M. Fabre, are peculiarly interesting.

The genus Sitaris (a small beetle allied to *Cantharis*, the blister-fly, and to the oil-beetle) is parasitic on a kind of bee (*Anthophora*) which excavates subterranean galleries, each leading to a cell.   The eggs of the sitaris,

which are deposited at the entrance of the galleries, are
hatched at the end of September or beginning of October, and M. Fabre not unnaturally expected that the
young larvæ, which are active little creatures with six
serviceable legs, would at once eat their way into the
cells of the anthophora.   No such thing : till the month
of April following they remained without leaving their
birth-place, and consequently without food; nor did
they in this long time change either in form or size.
M. Fabre ascertained this, not only by examining the
burrow of the anthophoras, but also by direct observations of some young larvæ kept in captivity.   In April,
however, his captives at last awoke from their long
lethargy, and hurried anxiously about their prisons.
Naturally inferring that they were in search of food,
M. Fabre supposed that this would consist either of the
larvæ or pupæ of the anthophora, or of the honey with
which it stores its cell.   All three were tried without
success. The first two were neglected, and the larvæ, when
placed on the latter, either hurried away or perished
in the attempt, being evidently unable to deal with the
sticky substance.   M. Fabre was in despair : "Jamais
expérience," he says, "n'a eprouvé pareille déconfiture.
Larves, nymphes, cellules, miel, je vous ai tous offert ;
que voulez-vous, donc, bestioles maudites ? "   The first
ray of light came to him from our countryman, Newport,
who ascertained that a small parasite found by Léon
Dufour on one of the wild bees was, in fact, the larva
of the oil-beetle.   The larvæ of sitaris much resembled
Dufour's larvæ.   Acting on this hint, M. Fabre examined many specimens of anthophora, and found on
them at last the larvæ of his sitaris.   The males of

anthophora emerge from the pupæ sooner than the
females, and M. Fabre ascertained that, as they come out
of their galleries, the little sitaris larvæ fasten upon
them. Not, however, for long : instinct teaches them
that they are not yet in the straight path of development ; and, watching their opportunity, they pass from
the male to the female bee. Guided by these indications, M. Fabre examined several cells of anthophora ;
in some, the egg of the anthophora floated by itself on
the surface of the honey : in others, on the egg, as on a
raft, sat the still more minute larva of the sitaris. The
mystery was solved. At the moment when the egg is
laid, the sitaris larva springs upon it. Even while the
poor mother is carefully fastening up her cell, her mortal
enemy is beginning to devour her offspring ; for the egg
of the anthophora serves not only as a raft, but as a
repast. The honey, which is enough for either, would
be too little for both ; and the sitaris, therefore, at its
first meal, relieves itself from its only rival. After eight
days the egg is consumed, and on the empty shell the
sitaris undergoes its first transformation, and makes its
appearance in a very different form.

The honey, which was fatal before, is now necessary,
the activity, which before was necessary, is now useless ;
consequently, with the change of skin, the active, slim
larva changes into a white, fleshy grub, so organized as
to float on the surface of the honey, with the mouth
beneath and the spiracles above the surface : " Grâce à
l'embonpoint du ventre," says M. Fabre, " la larve est à
l'abri de l'asphyxie." In this state it remains until the
honey is consumed ; then the animal contracts, and de-
taches itself from its skin, within which the further

transformations take place. In the next stage, which
M. Fabre calls the pseudo-chrysalis, the larva has a solid
corneous envelope and an oval shape, and in its colour,
consistency, and immobility, reminds one of a dipterous
pupa. The time passed in this condition varies much.
When it has elapsed, the animal moults again, again
changes its form ; after this it becomes a pupa, without
any remarkable peculiarities. Finally, after these wonderful ᴗhanges and adventures, in the month of August
the perfect beetle makes its ᴗppearance.

In fact, whenever in any group we find differences in
form or colour, we shall always find them associated with
differences in habit. Let us take the case of caterpillars.
The prevailing colour of caterpillars is green, like that
of leaves. The value of this to the young insect, the
protection it affords, are obvious. We must all have
observed how difficult it is to distinguish small green
caterpillars from the leaves on which they feed. When,
however, they become somewhat larger, their form be-
trays them, and it is important that there should be
certain marks to divert the eye from the outlines of the
body. This is effected, and much protection given, by
longitudinal lines (Fig. 38), which accordingly are found
on a great many caterpillars. These lines, both in colour
and thickness, much resemble some of the lines on leaves
(especially those, for instance, of grasses), and also the
streaks of shadow which occur among foliage. If, however, this be the explanation of them, then they ought
to be wanting, as a general rule, in very small caterpillars, and to prevail most among those which feed on
or among grasses. Now, similar lines occur on a great
number of caterpillars belonging to most different groups

of butterflies and moths, as you may see by turning over the illustrations of any monograph of the group. They exist among the hawk-moths, as, for instance, in the humming-bird hawk-moth; they occur in many butterflies, as, in *Arge galathea*, which feeds on the cat's-tail grass; and in many moths, as, for instance, in *Pyrophila tragopoginis*, which feeds on the leaves

FIG. 38.—*Arge galathea.*

of the "John Go-to-bed at Noon" (*Tragopogon*). But you will find that the smallest caterpillars rarely possess these white streaks. As regards the second point also, the streaks are generally wanting in caterpillars which feed on large-leaved plants. The *Satyridæ*, on the contrary, all possess them, and all live on grass. In fact we may say, as a general rule, that these longi-

tudinal streaks only occur on caterpillars which live on
or among narrow-leaved plants.   As the insect grows,
these lines often disappear on certain segments, and are
replaced by diagonal lines.   These diagonal lines (Fig.
39) occur in a great many caterpillars, belonging to the
most distinct families of butterflies and moths.   They
come off just at the same angle as the ribs of leaves, and
resemble them very much in general effect.   They occur
also especially in species which feed on large-leaved
plants, and I believe I may say that though a great
many species of caterpillars present these lines, they

Fig. 39.—*Smerinthus ocellatus.*

rarely, if ever, occur in species which live on grass;
while, on the contrary, they are very frequent in those
species which live on large-leaved plants.   It might at
first be objected to this view that there are many cases,
as in the elephant hawk-moth, in which caterpillars have
both.   A little consideration, however, will explain this.
In small caterpillars these oblique lines would be useless,
because they must have some relation, not only in colour,
but in their distance apart, to the ribs of the leaves.
Hence, while there are a great many species which have
longitudinal lines when young, and diagonal ones when
they are older and larger, there is not, I believe, a single

one which begins with diagonal lines, and then replaces
them with longitudinal ones.   The disappearance of the
longitudinal lines on those segments which have diagonal
ones, is striking, where the lines are marked.   It is an
advantage, because white lines crossing one another at
such an angle have no relation to anything which occurs
in plants, and would make the creature more conspicuous.   When, therefore, the diagonal lines are developed. the longitudinal ones often disappear.   There is
one other point in connection with these diagonal lines
to which I must call your attention.   In many species
they are white, but in some cases, as for instance in the
beautiful green caterpillar of the privet hawk-moth, the
white streak is accompanied by a coloured one—in that
case lilac.   At first we might think that this would be a
disadvantage, as tending to make the caterpillar more
conspicuous ; and in fact, if we put one in full view,
for instance, out on a table, and focus the eye on it, the
coloured lines are very striking.   But we must remember
that the habit of the insect is to sit on the lower side of
the leaf, generally near the midrib, and in the subdued
light of such a situation, especially if the eye be not
looking exactly at them, the coloured lines beautifully
simulate a line of soft shadow, such as must always
accompany a strong rib ; and I need not tell any artist
that the shadows of yellowish green must be purplish.
Moreover, any one who has ever found one of these
large caterpillars will, I am sure, agree with me that
it is surprising, when we consider their size and
conspicuous colouring, how difficult they are to see.

But though the prevailing colour of caterpillars is
green, there are numerous exceptions.   In one great

family of moths (the *Geometridæ*) the prevailing colour is brown. These caterpillars, however, escape observation by their great similarity to brown twigs, a resemblance which is heightened by their peculiar attitudes, and in many cases by the existence of warts or protuberances, which look like buds. Some, however, even of these caterpillars, when very young, are green. Again, some caterpillars are white. These either feed on and burrow in wood—such are, for instance, the species of *Sphecia*, *Trochilium*, and *Zeuzera*—or on roots, as the ghost-moth (*Hepialus humuli*). *Hipparchia hyperanthus* (the ringlet butterfly) also has whitish caterpillars, and this may at first sight appear to contradict the rule, since it feeds on grass. Its habit is, however, to keep at the roots by day, and feed only at night.

In various genera we find black caterpillars, which are of course very conspicuous, and, so far as I know, not distasteful to birds. In such cases, however, it will be found that they are covered with hairs or spines, which protect them from most birds. In these species, the bold dark colour may be an advantage, by rendering the hair more conspicuous. As instances of caterpillars which are black and hairy, I may quote, among our English butterflies, *Melitæa cinxia*, *M. artemis*, *M. athalia*, *M. selene*, *M. dia*, *M. euphrosyne*, *Argynnis aglaia*, *Vanessa polychloros*, *V. io*, and *V. antiope* ; while among moths, there are *Arctia villica*, *A. caja*, and *Heraclea dominula*. I do not know any large caterpillar which is black and smooth.

Brown caterpillars, also, are frequently protected by hairs or spines in the same way. As instances may be mentioned *Cynthia cardui*, *Argynnis lathonia*, *Erio-*

gaster lanestris, Odonestis potatoria, Lasiocampa rubi,
L. trifolii, and *L. roboris.* Brown caterpillars, however,
unlike black ones, are frequently naked. These fall into
two principal categories: firstly, those which, like the
Geometridæ, put themselves into peculiar and stiff
attitudes, so that in form, colour, and position they
closely resemble bits of dry stick; and, secondly, those
which feed on low plants, concealing themselves on the
ground by day, and only coming out in the dark.

Yellow and yellowish-green caterpillars are abundant,
and their colour is a protection. Red and blue, on the
contrary, are much less common colours, and are generally present as spots.

Moreover, caterpillars with red lines or spots are generally hairy, and this for the reason given above. Such
species, therefore, would be avoided by birds. There are
no doubt some apparent exceptions. *Papilio machaon,*
for instance, has red spots and still is smooth; but as it
emits a strongly-scented liquid when alarmed, it is
probably distasteful to birds. I cannot recall any other
case of a British caterpillar which has conspicuous red
spots or lines, and yet is smooth.

Blue is among caterpillars even a rarer colour than
red. Indeed, among our larger larvæ, the only cases I
can recall are the species of *Gastropacha,* which have
two conspicuous blue bands, the Death's-head moth,
which has broad diagonal bands, and *Chærocampa,*
which has two bright blue oval patches on the third
segment. The species of *Gastropacha* are protected by
being hairy, but why they have the blue bands I have
no idea. It is interesting, that the other species both
frequent plants which have blue flowers. The peculiar

hues of the Death's-head hawk-moth caterpillar, which feeds on the potato, unite so beautifully the brown of the earth, the yellow and green of the leaves, and the blue of the flowers, that, in spite of its size, it can scarcely be perceived unless the eye be focussed exactly upon it.

Chœrocampa nerii is also an interesting case. Many of the hawk-moth caterpillars have eye-like spots, to which I shall have to allude again presently. These are generally reddish or yellowish, but in *Ch. nerii*, which feeds on the periwinkle, they are bright blue, and in form as well as colour closely resemble the blue petals of that flower. *Ch. celerio* also has two smaller blue spots, with reference to which I can make no suggestion. It is a very rare species, and I have never seen it. Possibly, in this case, the blue spots may be an inherited character.

No one who looks at any representations of hawk-moth caterpillars can fail to be struck by the peculiar colouring of those belonging to the genus *Anceryx*, which differ in style of colouring from all other sphinx larvæ, having longitudinal bands of brown and green. Why is this? Their *habitat* is different. They feed on the leaves of the pinaster, and their peculiar colouring offers a general similarity to the brown twigs and narrow green leaves of a conifer. There are not many species of Lepidoptera which feed on the pine, but there are a few; such, for instance, are *Achatia spreta* and *Dendrolimus pini*, both of which have a very analogous style of colouring to that of *Anceryx*, while the latter has also tufts of bluish-green hair which singularly mimic the leaves of the pine. It is still more remarkable that in a different order of insects, that of the *Hymenoptera*, we again find species—for instance, *Lophyrus socia*—which live on the pine, and in which the same style of colouring is repeated.

Let us now take a single group, and see how far we can explain its various colours and markings, and what are the lessons which they teach us. For this purpose, I think I cannot do better than select the larvæ of the *Sphingidæ*, which have just been the subject of a masterly monograph by Dr. Weismann, from whom most of the following facts are taken.

The caterpillars of this group are very different in colour—green, white, yellow, brown, sometimes even gaudy, varied with spots, patches, streaks, and lines. Now, are these differences merely casual and accidental, or have they a meaning and a purpose? In many, perhaps in most cases, the markings serve for the purpose of concealment. When, indeed, we see caterpillars represented on a white sheet of paper, or if we put them on a plain table, and focus the eye on them, the colours and markings would seem, if possible, to render them even more conspicuous; as, for instance, in *Deilephila galii;* but amongst the intricate lines and varied colours of foliage and flowers, and if the insect be a little out of focus, the effect is very different.

Let us begin with the *Chærocampa elpenor*, the elephant hawk-moth. The caterpillars, as represented in most entomological works, are of two varieties, most of them brown (Fig. 46), but some green. Both have a white line on the three first segments; two remarkable eye-like spots on the fourth and fifth, and a very faint median line; and are rather more than four inches long. I will direct your attention specially, for the moment, to

three points :—What do the eye-spots and the faint
lateral line mean ? and why are some green, and some
brown, offering thus such a marked contrast to the leaves
of the *Epilobium parvum*, on which they feed ?   Other

FIG. 40.—*Chœrocampa elpenor.*   First stage.

questions will suggest themselves later.   I must now call
your attention to the fact that, when the caterpillars first
quit the egg, and come into the world (Fig. 40), they are
quite different in appearance, being, like so many other

FIG. 41.—*Chœrocampa elpenor.*   Second stage.

small caterpillars, bright green, and almost exactly the
colour of the leaves on which they feed.   That this colour
is not a necessary or direct consequence of the food, we
see from the case of quadrupeds, which, as I need scarcely

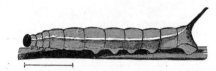

FIG. 42.—*Chœrocampa elpenor.*   Just before second moult.

say, are never green.   It is, however, so obviously a
protection to small caterpillars, that the explanation of
their green colour suggests itself to every one.   After
five or six days, and when they are about a quarter of

an inch in length, they go through their first moult.
In their second stage (Fig. 41), they have two white lines,
stretching along the body from the horn to the head;
and after a few days (Fig. 42), but not at first, traces
of the eye-spots appear on the fourth and fifth segments,
shown by a slight wave in the upper line. After

Fig. 43.—*Chærocampa elpenor.*   Third stage.

another five or six days, and when about half an
inch in length, our caterpillars moult again. In their
third stage (Fig. 43), the commencement of the eye-
spots is more marked, while, on the contrary, the lower
longitudinal line has disappeared. After another moult
(Fig. 44), the eye-spots are still more distinct, the white

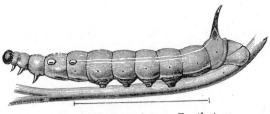

Fig. 44.—*Chærocampa elpenor.*   Fourth stage.

gradually becomes surrounded by a black line, while in
the next stage (Fig. 45) the centre becomes somewhat
violet. The white lines have almost, or entirely disappeared, and in some specimens, faint diagonal lines make
their appearance. Some few assume a brownish tint,
but not many. A fourth moult takes place in seven

or eight days, and when the caterpillars are about
an inch and a half in length. Now, the difference
shows itself still more between the two varieties, some
remaining green, while the majority become brown.
The eye-spots are more marked, and the pupil more

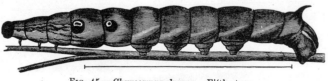

FIG. 45.—*Chœrocampa elpenor.* Fifth stage.

distinct, the diagonal lines plainer, while the white
line is only indicated on the first three, and on the
eleventh segment. The last stage (Fig. 46) has been
already described.

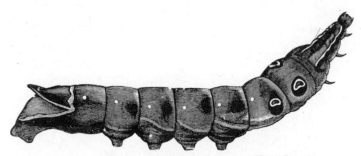

FIG. 46.—*Chœrocampa elpenor.* Full grown. (Natural size.)

Now, the principal points to which I desire to draw
attention are (1) the green colour, (2) the longitudinal
lines, (3) the diagonal lines, (4) the brown colour, and
(5) the eye-spots.

As regards the first three, however, I think I need
say no more. The value of the green colour to the
young larva is obvious; nor is it much less clear that

when the insect is somewhat larger, the longitudinal
lines are a great advantage, while subsequently diagonal
ones become even more important.

The next point is the colour of the mature caterpillars. We have seen that some are green, and others
brown. The green ones are obviously merely those
which have retained their original colour. Now for
the brown colour. This probably makes the caterpillar
even more conspicuous among the green leaves than
would otherwise be the case. Let us see, then,
whether the habits of the insect will throw any
light upon the riddle. What would you do if you
were a big caterpillar? Why, like most other de-
fenceless creatures, you would feed by night, and lie
concealed by day. So do these caterpillars. When
the morning light comes, they creep down the stem
of the food-plant, and lie concealed among the thick
herbage, and dry sticks and leaves, near the ground,
and it is obvious that under such circumstances the
brown colour really becomes a protection. It might
indeed be argued that the caterpillars, having become
brown, concealed themselves on the ground; and that
we were in fact reversing the state of things. But this
is not so; because, while we may say, as a general
rule, that (with some exceptions due to obvious causes)
large caterpillars feed by night and lie concealed by
day, it is by no means always the case that they are
brown; some of them still retaining the green colour.
We may then conclude that the habit of concealing
themselves by day came first, and that the brown
colour is a later adaptation. It is, moreover, interesting to note, that while the caterpillars which live on

low plants often go down to the ground, and turn
brown, those which feed on large trees or plants
remain on the under side of the leaves, and retain
their green colour.

Thus, in *Smerinthus ocellatus*, which feeds on the
willow and sallow; *S. populi*, which feeds on the
poplar; and *S. tiliæ*, which frequents the lime, the
caterpillars all remain green; while in those which
frequent low plants, such as the convolvulus hawk-
moth, which frequents the convolvulus; *Chærocampa
nerii*, which feeds in this country on the periwinkle;
Chærocampa celerio, Ch. elpenor, and *Ch. porcellus*,
which live on galium, most of the caterpillars turn
brown. There are, indeed, some caterpillars which are
brown, and still do not go down to the ground, as, for
instance, those of *Aspilatis aspersaria*, and indeed of
the *Geometridæ* generally. These caterpillars, however,
as already mentioned, place themselves in peculiar
attitudes, which, combined with their brown colour,
make them look almost exactly like bits of stick or
dead twigs.

The last of the five points to which I called your
attention was the eye-spots. In some cases, spots may
serve for concealment, by resembling the marks on dead
leaves. In *Deilephila hippophae*, which feeds on the
hippophae, or sea buckthorn, a grey-green plant, the
caterpillar also is a similar grey-green, and has, when
full grown, a single red spot on each side, which, as
Weismann suggests, at first sight much resembles in
colour and size one of the berries of hippophae. This
might, at first, be supposed to constitute a danger, and
therefore to be a disadvantage, but the seeds, though

present, are not ripe, and consequently are not touched
by birds. Again, in *Chærocampa tersa*, there is an eye-
spot on each segment, which mimics the flower of the
plant on which it feeds (*Spermacoce hyssopifolia*). White
spots, in some cases, also resemble the spots of light
which penetrate foliage. In other instances, however,
and, at any rate, in our elephant hawk-moth, the eye-
spots certainly render the insect more conspicuous.
Now in some cases, as Wallace has pointed out, this is
an advantage, rather than a drawback. Suppose that
from the nature of its food or any other cause, as, for
instance, from being covered with hair, a small green
caterpillar were very bitter, or in any way disagreeable
or dangerous as food, still, in the number of small green
caterpillars which birds love, it would be continually
swallowed by mistake. If, on the other hand, it had a
conspicuous and peculiar colour, its evil taste would serve
to protect it, because the birds would soon recognize and
avoid it, as Weir and others have proved experimentally.
I have already alluded to a case of this among the
hawk-moths in *Deilephila euphorbiæ*, which, feeding on
euphorbia, with its bitter milky juice, is very distasteful
to birds, and is thus actually protected by its bold and
striking colours. The spots on our elephant hawk-moth
caterpillar do not admit of this explanation, because the
insect is quite good to eat—I mean for birds. We must,
therefore, if possible, account for these spots in some
other way. There can, I think, be little doubt that
Weismann is right when he suggests that the eye-
spots actually protect the caterpillar, by frightening
its foes.

Every one must have observed that these large cater-

pillars, as for instance that of *Ch. porcellus* (Fig. 47),
have a sort of uncanny, poisonous appearance; that
they suggest a small thick snake or other evil beast, and
the so-called "eyes" do much to increase the deception.
Moreover, the ring on which they are placed is swollen,
and the insect, when in danger, has the habit of re-
tracting its head and front segments, which gives it an

FIG. 47.—*Chœrocampa porcellus.*

additional resemblance to some small reptile. That
small birds are, as a matter of fact, afraid of these caterpillars (which, however, I need not say, are in reality
altogether harmless) Weismann has proved by actual
experiment. He put one of these caterpillars in a tray,
in which he was accustomed to place seed for birds.
Soon a little flock of sparrows and other small birds
assembled to feed as usual. One of them lit on the
edge of this tray, and was just going to hop in, when
she spied the caterpillar. Immediately she began
bobbing her head up and down, but was afraid to go
nearer. Another joined her, and then another, until at
last there was a little company of ten or twelve birds,
all looking on in astonishment, but not one ventured
into the tray; while one bird, which lit in it unsuspect-
ingly, beat a hasty retreat in evident alarm as soon as
she perceived the caterpillar. After waiting for some
time, Weismann removed it, when the birds soon
attacked the seeds. Other caterpillars also are probably

protected by their curious resemblance to spotted snakes. One of the large Indian species has even acquired the power of hissing.

Moreover, as Weismann points out, we may learn another very interesting lesson from these caterpillars. They leave the egg, as we have seen, a plain green, like so many other caterpillars, and gradually acquire a succession of markings, the utility of which I have just attempted to explain. The young larva, in fact, represents an old form, and the species, in the lapse of ages, has gone through the stage which each individual now passes through in a few weeks. Thus the caterpillar of *Chærocampa porcellus*, the small elephant hawk-moth, a species very nearly allied to *Ch. elpenor*, passes through almost exactly the same stages as that of *Ch. elpenor*. But it leaves the egg with a subdorsal line, which the caterpillar of *Ch. elpenor* does not acquire until after its first moult. No one can doubt, however, that there was a time when the new-born caterpillars of *Ch. porcellus* were plain green, like those of *Ch. elpenor*. In this respect, then, *Ch. porcellus* is a newer specific form than *Ch. elpenor*. Again, if we compare the mature caterpillars of *Chærocampa*, we shall find there are some forms, such as *Ch. myron* and *Ch. chærilus*, which never develop eye-spots, but which, even when full grown, correspond to the second stage of *Ch. elpenor*. Here, then, we seem to have a species still in the stage which *Ch. elpenor* must have passed through long ago.

The genus *Deilephila*, of which we have in England three species—the euphorbia hawk-moth, the galium hawk-moth, and the rayed hawk-moth—is also very

instructive. The caterpillar of the euphorbia hawk-moth
begins life of a clear green colour, without a trace of
the subsequent markings. After the first moult, however, it has a number of black patches, a white line,
and a series of white dots, and has, therefore, at one
bound, acquired characters which in *Ch. elpenor*, as we
have seen, were only very gradually assumed. In the
third stage, the line has disappeared, leaving the white
spots. In the fourth, the caterpillars have become very
variable, but are generally much darker than before, and
have a number of white dots under the spots. In the
fifth stage, there is a second row of white spots under
the first. The caterpillars not being good to eat, there
is, as has been already pointed out, no need for, or
attempt at, concealment. Now, if we compare the
mature caterpillars of other species of the genus, we
shall find that they represent phases in the development
of *Deilephila euphorbiæ*. *D. hippophae*, for instance,
even when full grown, is a plain green, with only a
trace of the line, and corresponds, therefore, with a very
early stage of *D. euphorbiæ; D. zygophylli*, of South
Russia, has the line, and represents the second stage of
D. euphorbiæ; D. livornica has the line and the row
of spots, and represents therefore the third stage;
lastly, *D. vespertilio* and *D. galii* have progressed further,
and lost the longitudinal line, but they never acquire the
second row of spots which characterizes the last stage
of *D. euphorbiæ*.

Thus, then, the individual life of certain caterpillars
gives us a clue to the history of the species in past
ages.

For such inquiries as this, the larvæ of Lepidoptera

are particularly suitable, because they live an exposed
life; because the different species, even of the same genus,
often feed on different plants, and are therefore exposed to
different conditions ; and last, not least, because we know
more about the larvæ of the Lepidoptera than about those
of any other insects.   The larvæ of ants all live in
the dark ; they are fed by the perfect ants, and being
therefore all subject to very similar conditions, are all
very much alike.   It would puzzle even a good naturalist
to determine the species of an ant larva, while, as we
all know, the caterpillars of butterflies and moths are
as easy to distinguish as the perfect insects ; they differ
from one another as much as, sometimes more than, the
butterflies and moths themselves.

There are five principal types of colouring among
caterpillars.   Those which live inside wood, or leaves,
or underground, are generally of a uniform pale hue ;
the small leaf-eating caterpillars are green, like the leaves
on which they feed.   The other three types may, to
compare small things with great, be likened to the three
types of colouring among cats.   There are the ground
cats, such as the lion or puma, which are brownish or
sand colour, like the open places they frequent.   So also
caterpillars which conceal themselves by day at the
roots of their food-plant tend, as we have seen, even if
originally green, to assume the colour of earth.   Nor
must I omit to mention the *Geometridæ*, to which I have
already referred, and which, from their brown colour,
their peculiar attitudes, and the frequent presence of
warts or protuberances, closely mimic bits of dry stick.
That the caterpillars of these species were originally
green, we may infer from the fact that some of them

at least are still of that colour when first born. Then there are the spotted or eyed cats, such as the leopard, which live among trees ; and their peculiar colouring renders them less conspicuous by simulating spots of light which penetrate through foliage. So also many caterpillars are marked with spots, eyes, or patches of colour. Lastly, there are the jungle cats, of which the tiger is the typical species, and which have stripes, rendering them very difficult to see among the brown grass which they frequent. It may, perhaps, be said that this comparison fails, because the stripes of tigers are perpendicular, while those of caterpillars are either longitudinal or oblique. This, however, so far from constituting a real difference, confirms the explanation ; because in each case the direction of the lines follows that of the foliage. The tiger, walking horizontally on the ground, has transverse bars ; the caterpillar, clinging to the grass in a vertical position, has longitudinal lines ; while those which live on large-veined leaves have oblique lines, like the oblique ribs of the leaves.

It might, however, be suggested that the cases given above are exceptional. I have, therefore, in a paper read before the Entomological Society, tabulated all our larger British caterpillars, and the result is very interesting. As regards butterflies, we have sixty-six species, out of which eighteen are spiny, and two may fairly be called hairy. I do not speak of mere pubescence, but of true hairs and spines. Now, out of these twenty, ten are black, two greyish, six brown or brownish, one greyish-green, and only one (*L. sybilla*) green. Thus, while green is so preponderating a colour among smooth-skinned or ordinarily pubescent caterpillars (thirty-seven out of the sixty-six species of butterflies being of this colour), only a single spiny species is thus coloured.

Now, let us look at these numbers under a different aspect. Out of sixty-six species, ten are black: and, as we have already seen, all these are spiny or hairy. The larva of *Parnassius apollo*—a species reputed to have been taken in this country—is stated to be black, and is not hairy or spiny; but, as it has red spots and blue tubercles, and the neck is furnished with a yellow forked appendage, it is probably sufficiently protected. The larva of *Papilio machaon* is also marked with black, and provided with strongly-scented tentacles, which probably serve as a protection.

Again, there are sixteen brown species, and of these, seven are hairy or spiny.

Red and blue are rare colours among caterpillars. Omitting minute dots, we have six species, more or less marked with red or orange, viz., *A. aglaia*, *V. antiopa*, *N. lucina*, *C. alsus*, *P. cratægi*, and *P. machaon*. Of these, two are spiny, two hairy, and one protected by scent-emitting tentacles. The orange medio-dorsal line of *C. alsus* is not very conspicuous, and has been omitted in some descriptions. Blue is even rarer than red; in fact, none of our butterfly larvæ can be said to exhibit this colour.

Now, let us turn to the moths. Of these caterpillars, the *Sphingidæ*, *Cocliopidæ*, *Procridæ*, *Zygænidæ*, *Nolidæ*, *Lithosiidæ*, *Euchelidæ*, *Chelonidæ*, *Liparidæ*, *Bombycidæ*, *Drepanulæ*, and *Pseudo-Bombyces* are tabulated—these groups comprising nearly all our larger species. The *Hepialidæ*, *Zeuzeridæ*, and *Sesidæ* have been omitted, because these larvæ are all internal or

F

subterranean feeders, and are devoid of any striking
colour. This leaves 122 species, out of which sixty-
eight are hairy or downy ; and of these, forty-eight are
marked with black or grey, fifteen brown, or brownish,
two yellowish-green, one bluish-grey, one striped with
yellow and black, and one reddish-grey. Of the two
yellowish-green hairy species, which might be regarded
as exceptions, *Z. lonicerœ* is marked with black and
yellow, and *N. albulalis* is variable in colour, some
specimens of this caterpillar being orange. This last
species is also marked with black, so that neither of
these species can be considered of the green colour
which serves as a protection. Thus, among the moths
tabulated, there is not a single hairy species of the usual
green colour. On the other hand, there are fifty species
with black or blackish caterpillars, and of these, forty-
eight are hairy or downy.

In ten of our larger moths the caterpillars are more
or less marked with red. Of these, three are hairy, one
is an internal feeder, four have reddish lines, which
probably serve for protection by simulating lines of
shadow, and one (*D. euphorbiæ*) is inedible. The last,
D. livornica, is rare, and I have never seen the caterpillar ; but, to judge from figures, the reddish line and
spots would render it, not more, but less conspicuous
amongst the low herbage which it frequents.

Seven species only of our larger moths have any blue ;
of these four are hairy, the other three are hawk-moths.
In one (*A. atropos*) the violet colour of the side stripes
certainly renders the insect less conspicuous among the
flowers of the potato, on which it feeds. In *C. nerii*
there are two blue patches, which, both in colour and

form, curiously resemble the petals of the periwinkle, on which it feeds.   In the third species, *C. porcellus*, the bluish spots form the centres of the above-mentioned ocelli.

Among the *Geometridæ*, as already mentioned, the caterpillars are very often brown, and closely resemble bits of stick, the similarity being much increased by the peculiar attitudes they assume.   On the other hand, the large brown caterpillars of certain *Sphingidæ* are night feeders, concealing themselves on the ground by day; and it is remarkable that while species, such as *S. convolvuli*, which feed on low plants, turn brown as they increase in age and size ; others, like the *Smerinthi*, which frequent trees, and cannot therefore descend to the ground for concealment, remain green throughout life.   Omitting these, we find in the table, among the larger species, seventeen which are brown, of which twelve are hairy, and two have extensile caudal filaments.   The others, though not *Geometridæ*, closely resemble bits of stick, and place themselves in peculiar, and stiff attitudes.

And thus, summing up the caterpillars, both of butterflies and moths, out of the eighty-eight spiny and hairy species tabulated, only one is green (*L. sybilla*), and even this may not be protectively coloured, since it has yellow warts and white lateral lines.   On the other hand, a very great majority of the black and brown caterpillars, as well as those more or less marked with blue and red, are either hairy or spiny, or have some special protection.

Here, then, I think, we see reasons, for many at any rate of the variations of colour and ·markings in caterpillars, which at first sight seem so fantastic and inexplicable. I should, however, produce an impression very different from that which I wish to convey, were I to lead you to suppose that all these varieties have been explained, or are understood. Far from it; they still offer a large field for study; nevertheless I venture to think the evidence now brought forward, however imperfectly, is at least sufficient to justify the conclusion that there is not a hair or a line, not a spot or a colour, for which there is not a reason,—which has not a purpose or a meaning in the economy of nature.

ON THE HABITS OF ANTS.

I.

THE Anthropoid apes no doubt approach more nearly to Man in bodily structure than do any other animals ; but when we consider the habits of Ants, their social organ ization, their large communities, elaborate habitations, their roadways, their possession of domestic animals, and even, in some cases, of slaves, it must be admitted that they have a fair claim to rank next to man in the scale of intelligence. They present, moreover, not only a most interesting but also a very extensive field of study. In this country we have nearly thirty species ; but ants become more numerous, in species as well as individuals, in warmer countries, and more than seven hundred kinds are known. Even this large number is certainly far short of those actually in existence.

I have kept in captivity nearly half of our British species of ants, and at the present moment have in my room more than thirty nests, belonging to about twenty species ; some of which, however, are not English. No two species are identical in habits ; and, on various accounts, their mode of life is far from easy to unravel. In the first place, most of their time is passed under-ground : all the education of the young, for instance,

is carried on in the dark.   Again, ants are essentially
gregarious ; it is in some cases difficult to keep a few
alive by themselves in captivity, and at any rate their
habits under such circumstances are entirely altered.
If, on the other hand, a whole community be kept, then
the great number introduces a fresh element of difficulty
and complexity.   Moreover, within the same species,
the individuals seem to differ in character, and even
the same individual will behave very differently under
different circumstances.   Although, then, ants have attracted the attention of many naturalists, as Gould, De
Geer, Swammerdam, Latreille, Leeuwenhoek, and Huber,
and have recently been the object of interesting observations by Frederick Smith, Belt, Moggridge, Bates,
Mayr, Emery, Forel, and others, they still present one
of the most promising fields for observation and
experiment.

The larvæ of ants, like those of bees and wasps, are
small, white, legless grubs, somewhat conical in form,
narrow towards the head.   They are carefully tended
and fed, being carried about from chamber to chamber
by the workers, probably in order to secure the most
suitable amount of warmth and moisture.   I have
observed also that they are very often sorted according
to age.   It is sometimes very curious in my nests to see
the larvæ arranged in groups according to size, so that
they remind one of a school divided into five or six
classes.   When full grown, they turn into pupæ, sometimes naked, sometimes covered with a silken cocoon,
constituting the so-called "ant-eggs."   After remaining
some days in this state, they emerge as perfect insects.
In many cases, however, they would perish in the

attempt, if they were not assisted; and it is very pretty to see the older ants helping them to extricate themselves, carefully unfolding their legs and smoothing out their wings, with truly feminine tenderness and delicacy.

Under ordinary circumstances, an ants' nest, like a beehive, consists of three kinds of individuals ; workers, or imperfect females (which constitute the great majority), males, and perfect females. There are, however, often several queens in an ants' nest ; while, as we all know, there is never more than one in a hive. The ant queens have wings, but after a single flight they tear off their own wings, and do not again quit the nest. In addition to the ordinary workers, there is in some species a second, or rather a third, form of female. In almost any ants' nest, we may see that the workers differ more or less in size. The amount of difference, however, depends upon the species. In *Lasius niger*, the small brown garden ant, the workers are, for instance, much more uniform than in the little yellow meadow ant, or in *Atta barbara*, where some of them are more than twice as large as others. But in certain ants there are differences still more remarkable. Thus, in a Mexican species, besides the common workers, which have the form of ordinary neuter ants, there are certain others, in which the abdomen is swollen into an immense subdiaphanous sphere. These individuals are very inactive, and principally occupied in elaborating a kind of honey.[1] In the genus *Pheidole*, very common in southern Europe, there are also two distinct forms of workers without any intermediate gradations ; one with heads of the usual

[1] Westwood, *Modern Classification of Insects*, vol. ii. p. 225.

proportion, and a second with immense heads, provided
with very large jaws. These latter are generally supposed to act as soldiers, and the size of the head enables
the muscles which move the jaws to be of unusual
dimensions : the little workers are also very pugnacious.
This differentiation of certain individuals, so as to adapt
them to special functions, seems to me very remarkable ;
for it must be remembered that the difference is not one
of age or sex.

The food of ants consists of insects, great numbers of
which they destroy ; of honey, honeydew, and fruit ;

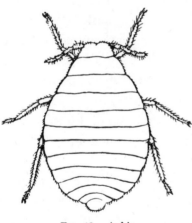

FIG. 48.—Aphis.

indeed, scarcely any
animal or sweet sub-
stance comes amiss to
them. Some species,
such, for instance, as
the small brown garden
ant, ascend bushes in
search of aphides. The
ant then taps the aphis
gently with her anten-
næ, and the aphis emits
a drop of sweet fluid,
which the ant drinks.
Sometimes the ants even build covered ways up to and
over the aphides, which, moreover, they protect from
the attacks of other insects. Our English ants do not
collect provision for the winter ; indeed, their food is
not of a nature which would admit of this. Some
southern species, however, collect grain, occasionally in
considerable quantities. Moreover, though our English
ants cannot be said exactly to lay up stores, some at

least do take steps to provide themselves with food in the future. The small yellow meadow ant (*Lasius flavus*), for instance, lives principally on the honeydew of certain aphides which suck the roots of grass. The ants collect the aphides in the nest, not only watching over them themselves, but, as I have been able to satisfy myself, even over their eggs; an act which one is much tempted to refer to forethought, and which in such a case implies a degree of prudence superior to that of some savages.

Besides these aphides, many other insects live in ants' nests. If they are to be regarded as domestic animals, then ants have more domestic animals than we have. The majority of these ant-guests are beetles. Some of them, as, for instance, the curious little *Claviger*, are quite blind, and are only found in ants' nests, the ants taking just as much care of them as of their own young It is evident, therefore, that in some way they are useful or agreeable to the ants. The subject, however, is one as yet but little understood, and very difficult to study. Grimm and Lespés consider that some of these beetles secrete a sweet fluid, as do the aphides, and from analogy this seems probable. Other creatures which habitually live in ants' nests, like the little *Beckia albinos*, or the blind woodlouse (*Platyarthrus*), perhaps make themselves useful as scavengers.

Nor are ants without their enemies. In addition to birds and other larger foes, if you disturb a nest of the brown ants at any time during the summer, you will probably see some very small flies hovering over them, and every now and then making a dash at some particular ant. These flies belong to the genus *Phora*, and to a species hitherto unnamed, which Mr. Verrall has been good enough to describe for me. They lay their eggs on the ants, inside which the larvæ live. Other species of the genus are in the same way parasitic on bees. In one case I observed that one of my ants had a mite attached to the under side of her head. The mite, which remained continuously in the same position, was almost as large as the head. The ant could not remove it herself. She did not come out of the nest, so that I could not do it for her, and none of her own companions for three months, during which I watched her, thought of performing this kind office.

In character the different species of ants differ very much from one another. *F. fusca*, the one which is pre-eminently the enslaved ant, is, as might be expected, extremely timid; while the nearly allied *F. cinerea* has, on the contrary, a considerable amount of individual audacity. *F. rufa*, the horse ant, according to M. Forel, is especially characterized by the want of individual initiative, and always moves in troops; he also regards the genus *Formica* as the most brilliant, though some others excel it in other respects; for instance, in the sharpness of their senses. *F. pratensis* worries its slain enemies; *F. sanguinea* never does. The slave-making ant (*P. rufescens*) is, perhaps, the bravest of all. If a single individual finds herself surrounded by enemies, she never attempts to fly, as any other ant would, but transfixes her opponents one after another, springing right and left with great agility, till at length she succumbs, overpowered by numbers. *M. scabrinodis* is cowardly and thievish; during wars among the larger species, they haunt the battle-fields and devour the dead. *Tetramorium* is said to be very greedy; *Myrmecina* very phlegmatic.

In industry, ants are not surpassed even by bees and wasps. They work all day, and in warm weather, if need be, even at night too. I once watched an ant from six in the morning, and she worked without intermission till a quarter to ten at night. I had put her to a saucer containing larvæ, and in this time she carried off no less than a hundred and eighty-seven to the nest. I once had another ant, which I employed in my experiments, under observation several days. Before I came up to London in the morning, and when I went to bed at night, I used to put her in a small bottle, but the moment she was let out she began to work again. On one occasion I was away from home for a week. On my return I let her out of the bottle, placing her on a little heap of larvæ, about three feet from the nest. Under these circumstances, I certainly did not expect her to work. However, though she had thus been six days in confinement, the brave little creature immediately picked up a larva, carried it off to the nest, and after half an hour's rest returned for another.

We have hitherto very little information as to the length of life in ants. So far, indeed, as the preparatory stages are concerned, we know that while they take only a few weeks in summer, in some species, as our small yellow meadow ants, the autumn larvæ remain with comparatively little change throughout the winter. It is much more difficult to ascertain the length of life of the perfect insect. It has, however, generally been supposed that they live about a season, and this is perhaps generally the case; but I have had workers of *Formica*

cinerea, F. fusca, and *Lasius niger* which lived in my
nests for as much as seven years. Of the identity
there could be no doubt, because as there was no queen
in the nest, no new workers were produced. I also
kept two queens of *Formica fusca* for a still longer
period. They were taken in December, 1874, and lived
with me till July, 1887, and August, 1888, respectively.
They must of course have been born at latest in the
spring of 1874, and the elder one must therefore
have been nearly fifteen years old at the time of
her death.

The behaviour of ants to one another differs very much,
according as they are alone or supported by numerous
companions. An ant which would run away in the first
case, will fight bravely in the second.

It is hardly necessary to say that, as a general rule,
each species lives by itself. There are, however, some interesting exceptions. The little *Stenamma Westwoodii*
is found exclusively in the nests of the much larger *F.
rufa,* and the allied *F. pratensis.* We do not know
what the relations between the two species are. The
Stenammas, however, follow the *Formicas* when they
change their nest, running about among them and
between their legs, tapping them inquisitively with their
antennæ, and even sometimes climbing on to their
backs, as if for a ride, while the large ants seem to take
little notice of them. They almost seem to be the dogs,
or perhaps rather cats, of the ants. Another small
species, *Solenopsis fugax,* which makes its chambers
and galleries in the walls of the nests of larger species,
is the bitter enemy of its hosts. The latter cannot get
at the foe, being too large to enter the galleries. The

little *Solenopsis*, therefore, are quite safe, and, as it appears, make incursions into the nurseries of the larger ant, and carry off the larvæ as food. It is as if we had small dwarfs, about eighteen inches to two feet long, harbouring in the walls of our houses, and every now and then carrying off some of our children into their horrid dens.

Most ants, indeed, will carry off the larvæ and pupæ of others if they get a chance; and this explains, or at any rate throws some light upon, that most remarkable phenomenon, the existence of slavery among ants. If you place a number of larvæ or pupæ in front of a nest of the horse ant, for instance, they are soon carried off; and those which are not immediately required for food remain alive for some days, though I have never been able to satisfy myself whether they are fed by their captors. Both the horse ant and the slave ant (*F. fusca*) are abundant species, and it must not unfrequently occur that the former, being pressed for food, attack the latter and carry off some of their larvæ and pupæ. Under these circumstances, it occasionally happens that the pupæ come to maturity in the nests of the horse ant; and nests are sometimes, though rarely, found, in which, with the legitimate owners, there are a few *F. fuscas*. With the horse ant this is, however, a very rare and exceptional phenomenon; but, with an allied species, *F. sanguinea*, a species which exists in our southern counties and throughout Europe, it has become an established habit. The *F. sanguineas* make periodical expeditions, attack neighbouring nests of *F. fusca*, and carry off the pupæ. When the latter come to maturity, they find themselves in a nest consisting partly of *F.*

sanguineas, partly of *F. fuscas*, the results of previous expeditions. They adapt themselves to circumstances, assist in the ordinary household duties, and, having no young of their own species, feed and attend those of the *F. sanguineas*. But though the *F. sanguineas* are thus aided by the *F. fuscas*, they have not themselves lost the instinct of working. It seems not improbable that there is some division of functions between the two species, but we have as yet no distinct knowledge on this point; and at any rate the *F. sanguineas* can "do" for themselves, and carry on a nest, if necessary, without slaves.

In another species, however, *Polyergus rufescens* (which is not British), this is not the case. They present a striking lesson of the degrading tendency of slavery, for they have become entirely dependent on their slaves. Even their bodily structure has undergone a change : their mandibles have lost their teeth, and have become mere nippers, deadly weapons indeed, but useless except in war. They have lost the greater part of their instincts : their art—that is, the power of build-ing ; their domestic habits—for they take no care of their own young, all this being done by the slaves ; their in-dustry—they take no part in providing the daily sup-plies ; if the colony changes the situation of its nest, the masters are all carried by the slaves to the new one ; nay, they have even lost the habit of feeding. Huber placed thirty of them with some larvæ and pupæ and a supply of honey in a box.

"At first," he says, "they appeared to pay some little attention to the larvæ ; they carried them here and there, but presently replaced them. More than one-half of the Amazons died of hunger in less than two days. They had not even traced out a dwelling, and the few ants still in existence were languid and without strength. I commiserated their condition, and gave them one of their black companions. This individual, unassisted, established order, formed a chamber in the earth, gathered together the larvæ, extricated several young ants that were ready to quit the condition of pupæ, and preserved the life of the remianing Amazons." [1]

This observation has been fully confirmed by other naturalists. However small the prison, however large the quantity of food, these stupid creatures will starve in the midst of plenty, rather than feed themselves. I have had a nest of this species under observation for a long time, but never saw one of the masters feeding. I have kept isolated specimens for weeks by giving them a slave for an hour or two a day to clean and feed them, and under these circumstances they remained in perfect health, while, but for the slaves, they would have perished in two or three days. I know no other case in nature of a species having lost the instinct of feeding.

In *P. rufescens*, the so-called workers, though thus helpless and stupid, are numerous, energetic, and in some respects even brilliant. In another slave-making species, however, *Strongylognathus*, the workers are much less numerous, and so weak that it is an unsolved problem how they contrive to make slaves.

Lastly, in a fourth species, *Anergates atratulus*, the workers are absent, the males and females living in nests with workers belonging to another ant, *Tetramorium cæspitum*. In these cases the *Tetramoriums*, having no queen, and consequently no young of their own, tend the young of the *Anergates*. It is therefore a case

---

[1] Huber, *Natural History of Ants.*

analogous to that of *Polyergus*, but it is one in which slave-owning has almost degenerated into parasitism. It is not, however, a case of true parasitism, because the *Tetramoriums* take great care of the *Anergates*, and if the nest is disturbed, carry them off to a place of safety.

M. Forel, in his excellent work on ants, has pointed out that very young ants devote themselves at first to the care of the larvæ and pupæ, and that they take no share in the defence of the nest or other out-of-door work until they are some days old. This seems natural, because at first their skin is comparatively soft; and it would clearly be undesirable to undertake rough work, or run into danger, until their armour had had time to harden. There are, however, reasons for thinking that the division of labour is carried still further. I do not allude merely to those cases in which there are completely different kinds of workers, but even to the ordinary workers. In *L. flavus*, for instance, it seems probable that the duties of the small workers are somewhat different from those of the large ones, though no such division of labour has yet been detected.

One of the most interesting problems with reference to ants is, of course, to determine the amount of their intelligence. In order to test this, it seemed to me that one way would be to ascertain some object which they would clearly desire, and then to interpose an obstacle which a little ingenuity would enable them to overcome. With this object in view, I placed food in a porcelain cup on a slip of glass surrounded by water, but accessible to the ants by a bridge, consisting of a strip of paper two-thirds of an inch long and one-third wide. Having then put a *F. nigra* from one of my nests to this food, she began carrying it off, and by degrees a number of friends came to help her. When about twenty-five ants were so engaged, I moved the little paper bridge slightly, so as to leave a chasm just so wide that the ants could not reach across. They came to the edge and tried hard to get over, but it did not occur to them to push the paper bridge, though the distance was only about one-third of an inch, and they might easily have done so. After trying for about a quarter of an hour they gave up the attempt, and returned home. This I repeated several times. Then, thinking that paper was a substance to which they were not accustomed, I tried the same with a bit of straw one inch long and one-eighth of an inch wide. The result was the same. I repeated this twice. Again I placed particles of food close to and directly over the nest, but connected with it only by a passage several feet in length. Under these circumstances it would be obviously a saving of time and labour to drop the food on to the nest, or at any rate to spring down with it, so as to save one journey. But though I have frequently tried the experiment, my ants never adopted either of these courses. I arranged matters so that the glass on which the food was placed was only raised one-third of an inch above the nest. The ants tried to reach down, and the distance was so small that occasionally, if another ant passed underneath just as one was reaching down, the upper one could step on to its back, and so descend; but this only happened accidentally, and they did not think of throwing the particles down, nor, which surprised me very much, would they jump down themselves. I then placed a heap of fine mould close to the glass, but just so far that they could still not reach across. It would have been quite easy for any ant, by moving a particle of earth for a quarter of an inch, to have made a bridge by which the food might have been reached, but this simple expedient did not occur to them. On the other hand, I then put some provisions in a shallow box with a glass top, and a single hole on one side, and put some specimens of *Lasius niger* to the food. As soon as a stream of ants was at work, busily carrying supplies off to the nest, and when they had got to know the way thoroughly, I poured some fine mould in front of the hole, so as to cover it up to a depth of about half an inch. I then took out the ants which were actually in the box. As soon as they had recovered from the shock of this unexpected proceeding on my part, they began to run all round and about the box, looking for some other place of entrance. Finding none, however, after a while they dug down into the earth just over the hole, carrying off the grains of earth one by one, and depositing them, without any order, all round at a distance of from half an inch to six inches, until they had excavated down to the doorway, when they again began carrying off the food as before. This experiment I repeated several times, always with the same result.

Again, I suspended some honey over a nest of *Lasius flavus*, at a height of about half an inch, and accessible only by a paper bridge more than ten feet long. Under the glass I then placed a small heap of earth. The ants soon swarmed over the earth on to the glass, and began feeding on the honey. I then removed a little of the earth,

so that there was an interval of about one-third of an inch
between the glass and the earth; but, though the distance was so small, the ants would not jump down, but
preferred to go round by the long bridge. They tried in
vain to stretch up from the earth to the glass, which,
however, was just out of their reach, though they could
touch it with their antennæ; but it did not occur to
them to heap the earth up a little; though, if they
had moved only half a dozen particles, they would
have secured for themselves direct access to the food.
This, however, appeared never to occur to them. At
length they gave up all attempts to reach up to the glass,
and went round by the long paper bridge. I left the
arrangement for several weeks, but they continued to do
the same.

Again I varied the experiment, as follows :—Having
left a nest without food for a short time, I placed some
honey on a small wooden brick, surrounded by a little
moat of glycerine, about half an inch wide and about $\frac{1}{10}$th
of an inch in depth. Over this moat I placed a paper
bridge, one end of which rested on some fine mould. I
then put an ant to the honey, and soon a little crowd
was collected round it. I then removed the paper
bridge; the ants could not cross the glycerine, they came
to the edge and walked round and round, but were unable
to get across; nor did it occur to them to make a bridge
or bank across the glycerine by means of the mould which
I had placed so conveniently for them. I was the more
surprised at this, on account of the ingenuity with which
they avail themselves of earth in constructing their
nests. For instance, wishing, if possible, to avoid the
trouble of frequently moistening the earth in my nests,

I supplied one of my ant-nests of *Lasius flavus* with a frame, containing, instead of earth, a piece of linen, one portion of which projected beyond the frame, and was immersed in water. The linen sucked up the water by capillary attraction, and thus the air in the frame was kept moist. The ants approved of this arrangement, and took up their quarters in the frame. To minimize evaporation, I usually closed the frames all round, leaving only one or two small openings for the ants, but in this case I left the outer side of the frame open. The ants, however, did not like being thus exposed ; they therefore brought earth from some little distance, and built up a regular wall along the open side, blocking up the space between the upper and lower plates of glass, and leaving only one or two small openings for themselves. This struck me as very ingenious. The same expedient was, moreover, repeated under similar circumstances by the slaves belonging to my nest of *Polyergus*.

I have also made many experiments on the power possessed by ants of remembering their friends. It will be recollected that Huber gives a most interesting ac-count of the behaviour of some ants, which, after being separated for four months, when brought together again, immediately recognized one another, and " fell to mutual caresses with their antennæ." Forel, however, regards these movements as having indicated fear and surprise rather than affection, though he also is quite inclined to believe, from his own observation, that ants would re-cognize one another after a separation of some months. The observation recorded by Huber was made casually ; and neither he nor any one else seems to have taken any steps to test it by subsequent experiments. The fact is

one, however, of so much interest, that it seemed to me
desirable to make further experiments on the subject.
On the 4th of August, 1875, therefore, I separated one
of my nests of *F. fusca* into two halves, which I kept
entirely apart.

I then from time to time put an ant from one of these
nests into the other, introducing also a stranger at the
same time. The stranger was always driven out, or
even killed. The friend, on the contrary, was never
attacked, though I am bound to say that I could see no
signs of any general welcome, or any especial notice
taken of her.

I will not trouble you with all the evidence, but will
content myself with one or two cases.

On the 12th November last, that is to say, after the
ants had been separated for a year and three months, I
put a friend and a stranger into one of the divisions.
The friend seemed quite at home. One of the ants at
once seized the stranger by an antenna, and began
dragging her about. At 11.45 the friend was quite at
home with the rest. The stranger was being dragged
about.

12.0. The friend was all right. Three ants now had
hold of the stranger by her legs and an antenna.

12.15, Do. do. 12.30, Do. do. 12.45, Do. do. 1.0,
Do. do. 1.30, Do. One now took hold of the friend,
but soon seemed to find out her mistake and let go
again. 1.45. The friend was all right. The stranger
was being attacked. The friend had also been almost
cleaned, while on the stranger the colour had been
scarcely touched. 2.15. Two ants were licking the
friend, while another pair was holding the stranger by

her legs. 2.20. The friend was now almost clean, so that I could only just perceive any colour. The stranger, on the contrary, was almost as much coloured as ever. She was now near the door, and I think would have come out, but two ants met and seized her. 3.0. Two ants were attacking the stranger. The friend was no longer distinguishable from the rest. 3.30, Do. 4.0, Do. 5.0, Do. 6.0. The stranger now escaped from the nest, and I put her back among her own friends.

The difference of behaviour was therefore most marked. The friends were gradually licked clean, and except for a few moments, and that evidently by mistake, were never attacked. The strangers, on the contrary, were not cleaned, were at once seized, dragged about either by one, two, or three assailants, and at length either made their escape from the nest, or were killed.

It is certainly most remarkable that ants should thus recognize their friends, after an interval of more than a year. I have since repeated these experiments with similar results.

Thus, I separated a nest of *F. fusca* into two portions, on the 20th October, 1876, and kept them entirely separate.

On the 25th February, 1877, at 8 a.m., I put an ant from the smaller lot back among her old companions. At 8.30 she was quite comfortably established among them. At 9, ditto. At 12, ditto, and at 4, ditto.

June 8th.—I put two specimens from the smaller lot back, as before, among their old friends. At 1, they were all right among the others. At 2, ditto. After this I could not distinguish them among the rest, but they were certainly not attacked.

June 9th.—Put in two more at the same hour. Up to 3 in the afternoon they were neither of them attacked. On the other hand, two strangers from different nests, whom I introduced at the same time, were both very soon attacked.

July 14th.—I put in two more of the friends at 10.15. In a few minutes they joined the others, and seemed quite at home. At 11, they were among the others ; at 12, ditto ; and at 1, ditto.

July 21st.—At 10.15 I put in two more of the old friends. At 10.30 neither were being attacked. At 11, ditto. 12, ditto. 2, ditto. 4, ditto. 6, ditto.

October 7th.—At 9.30 I put in two, and watched them carefully till 1. They joined the other ants, and were not attacked. I also put in a stranger from another nest. Her behaviour was quite different. She kept away from the rest, running off at once in evident fear, and kept wandering about, seeking to escape. At 10.30 she got out. I put her back, but she soon escaped again. I then put in another stranger. She was almost immediately attacked. In the meantime, the old friends were gradually cleaned. At 1.30 they could scarcely be distinguished. They seemed quite at home, while the stranger was being dragged about. After 2, I could no longer distinguish the friends. They were however certainly not attacked. The stranger, on the contrary, was killed and brought out of the nest.

This case, therefore, entirely confirmed the preceding ; while strangers were attacked, friends were amicably received.

In most species of ants, the power of smell is very keen. I placed ants on a strip of paper, each end of which was supported on a pin, the foot of which was immersed in water. They ran backwards and forwards along the paper, trying to escape. If then a camel's-hair pencil was suspended just over the paper, they passed under it without taking any notice of it ; but if it was scented, say with lavender-water, they at once stopped when they came near it, showing in the most unmistakable manner that they perceived the odour. This sense appears to reside, though not perhaps exclusively, in the antennæ. I tethered, for instance, a large specimen of *Formica ligniperda* with a fine thread to a board, and when she was quite quiet I approached a scented camel's-hair pencil slowly to the tip of the antenna, which was at once withdrawn, though the insect took no notice of a similar pencil, if not scented.

On the other hand, as regards their sense of hearing, the case is very different. Approaching an ant which was standing quietly, I have over and over again made the loudest and most shrill noises I could, using a penny pipe, a dog-whistle, a violin, as well as the most piercing and startling sounds I could produce with my own voice, without effect. At the same time I by no means would infer from this that they are really deaf, though it certainly seems that their range of hearing is very different from ours. We know that certain allied insects produce a noise by rubbing one of their abdominal rings against another. Landois is of opinion that ants also make sounds in the same way, though these sounds are inaudible to us. Our range is, however, after all, very limited, and the universe is probably full of music

which we cannot perceive.   There are, moreover, in the
antennæ of ants certain curious organs which may
perhaps be of an auditory character.   There are from
ten to a dozen in the terminal segment of *Lasius flavus*,
the small meadow ant, and indeed in most of the species
which I have examined ; and one or two in each of the
short intermediate segments.   These organs consist of
three parts : a small spherical cup opening to the outside,
a long narrow tube, and a hollow body, shaped like an
elongated clock-weight.   They may serve to increase the
resonance of sounds, acting in fact, to use the words of
Professor Tyndall, who was good enough to look at them
with me, like microscopic stethoscopes.

The organs of vision are in most ants very complex
and conspicuous.   There are generally three ocelli
arranged in a triangle on the top of their heads, and
on each side a large compound eye.

The mode in which the eyes act is by no means understood.   They consist of a number of facets, varying from
1—5 in *Ponera contracta*, to more than 1,000 in each eye
—as, for instance, in the males of *F. pratensis*.   In fact
these, so far fortunate, insects realize the wish of the poet :

> Thou lookest on the stars, my love ;
>   Ah, would that I could be
> Yon starry skies with thousand eyes,
>   That I might look on thee.

But if the male of *F. pratensis* sees 1,000 images
of the queen at once, this would seem to be a bewil-
dering privilege, and the prevailing opinion among
entomologists is that each facet only takes in a portion
of the field of view.

However this may be, the sight of ants does not seem

to be very good.   In order to test how far they are guided
by vision, I made the following experiments.   I placed
a common lead-pencil on a board, fastening it upright,
so as to serve as a landmark.   At the base I placed
a glass containing food, and put a *L. niger* to the
food ; when she knew her way from the glass to the nest
and back again perfectly well, she went quite straight
backwards and forwards.   I then took an opportunity
when the ant was on the glass, and moved the glass
with the ant on it about three inches.   Now, under
such circumstances, if she had been much guided by
sight, she could not of course have had any difficulty
in finding her way to the nest.   As a matter of fact,
however, she was entirely at sea, and after wandering
about for some time, got back to the nest by another
and very roundabout route.   I then again varied the
experiment as follows.   I placed the food in a small
china cup on the top of the pencil, which thus formed
a column seven and a half inches high.   When the
ant once knew her way, she went very straight to and
from the food.   I then moved the pencil six inches.   This
puzzled her very much : she went over and over the
spot where the pencil had previously stood, retraced
her steps several times almost to the nest, and then
returned along the whole line, showing great persever-
ance, if not much power of vision.   She found it at last,
but only after many meanderings.

I repeated the observation on three other ants with
the same result : the second was seven minutes before she
found the pencil, and at last seemed to do so accidentally ;
the third actually wandered about for no less than half
an hour, returning up the paper bridge several times.

Let us compare this relatively to man. An ant measuring, say one-sixth of an inch, and the pencil being seven inches high, it is consequently forty-two times as long as the ant. It bears, therefore, somewhat the same relation to the ant as a column two hundred and fifty feet high does to a man. The pencil having been moved six inches, it is as if a man in a country he knew well would be puzzled at being moved a few hundred feet; or, if put down in a square containing less than an acre, could not find a column two hundred and fifty feet high; that is to say, higher than the Duke of York's column.

As additional evidence I may adduce the fact, that when my *L. nigers* were carrying off food placed in a cup on a piece of board, if I turned the board round, so that the side which had been turned towards the nest was away from it, and *vice versâ*, the ants always returned over the same track on the board, and consequently directly away from home. If I moved the board to the other side of my artificial nest, the result was the same. Evidently they followed the track, not the direction.

It is remarkable, that notwithstanding the labours of so many excellent observers, and though ants swarm in every field and every wood, we do not yet know how their nests commence.

Three principal modes have been suggested :—after the marriage flight the young queen may either

1. Join her own or some other old nest;
2. Associate herself with a certain number of workers, and with their assistance commence a new nest; or

3. Found a new nest by herself.

The question can, of course, only be settled by observation, and the experiments made to determine it have
hitherto been indecisive.   Blanchard indeed, in his
work on the *Metamorphoses of Insects* (I quote from
Dr. Duncan's translation, p. 205), says, "Huber observed
a solitary female go down into a small underground
hole, take off her own wings, and become, as it were,
a worker; then she constructed a small nest, laid a
few eggs, and brought up the larvæ by acting as
mother and nurse at the same time."

This however is not quite a correct version of what
Huber says. His words are : " I enclosed several females
in a nest full of light humid earth, with which they
constructed lodges, where they resided; some singly,
others in common.   They laid their eggs and took
great care of them ; and notwithstanding the inconvenience of not being able to vary the temperature
of their habitation, they reared some, which became
larvæ of a tolerable size, but which soon perished
from the effect of my own negligence."

It will be observed that it was the eggs—not the
larvæ — which, according to Huber, these isolated
females reared. It is true that he attributes the early
and uniform death of the larvæ to his own negligence ;
but the fact remains, that in none of his observations
did an isolated female bring her offspring to maturity.
Other entomologists, especially Forel and Ebrard, have
repeated the same observations, with similar results ;
and as yet in no single case has an isolated female
been known to bring her young to maturity.   Forel
even thought himself justified in concluding from his

observations, and those of Ebrard, that such a fact could not occur. Lepeletier de St. Fargeau was of opinion that ants' nests originate in the second mode indicated above, and it is indeed far from improbable that this may occur. No clear case has, however, yet been observed.

Under these circumstances, I made various experiments, in order if possible to solve the question. For instance, I took an old fertile queen from a nest of *Lasius flavus*, and put her to another nest of the same species. The workers became very excited and killed her. I repeated the experiment, with the same result, more than once.

I conclude then, that, at any rate in the case of *Lasius flavus*, the workers will not adopt an old queen from another nest.

The following facts show that whether ants' nests sometimes originate in the two former modes or not, at any rate in some cases isolated queen ants are capable of giving origin to a new community. On the 14th August, 1876, I isolated two pairs of *Myrmica ruginodis*, which I found flying in my garden. I placed them with damp earth, food, and water, and they continued perfectly healthy through the winter. In April, however, one of the males died, and the second in the middle of May. The first eggs were laid between the 12th and 23rd April. They began to hatch, the first week in June, and the first larva turned into a chrysalis on the 27th; a second on the 30th; a third on the 1st of July, when there were also seven larvæ and two eggs. On the 8th there was another egg. On the 8th July a fourth larva had turned into a pupa. On

the 11th July I found there were six eggs, and on the
14th, about ten.   On the 15th, one of the pupæ began
to turn brown ; and the eggs were about fifteen in
number.   On the 16th, a second pupa began to turn
brown.   On the 21st, a fifth larva had turned into a
pupa, and there were about twenty eggs.   On the
22nd July, the first worker emerged, and a sixth larva
had changed.   On the 25th, when I looked into the
nest, I observed the young worker carrying the larvæ
about.   A   second   worker   was   coming   out.   On
July 28th, a third worker emerged, and a fourth on
the 5th August.   The eggs appeared less numerous,
some having probably been devoured.

This experiment shows that the queens of *Myrmica
ruginodis* have the instinct of bringing up larvæ, and
the power of founding communities.

The workers remained about six weeks in the egg, a
month in the state of larva, and 25—27 days as pupæ.

A nest of ants must not be confused with an ant
hill in the ordinary sense.   Very often indeed a nest
has only one dwelling, and in most species seldom more
than three or four.   Some communities, however, form
numerous colonies.   M. Forel even found a case in which
one nest of *F. exsecta* had no less than two hundred
colonies, and occupied a circular space with a radius of
nearly two hundred yards.   Within this area they had
exterminated all the other ants, except a few nests of
Tapinoma erraticum, which survived, thanks to the
great agility of this species.   In these cases, the number
of ants thus associated together must have been enormous. Even in single nests, Forel estimates the numbers
at from five thousand to half a million.

In their modes of fighting, different species of ants have their several peculiarities. Some also are much less military than others. *Myrmecina Latreillii*, for instance, never attack, and scarcely even defend themselves. Their skin is very hard, and they roll themselves into a ball, not defending themselves, even if their nest be invaded ; to prevent which, however, they make the entrances small, and often station at each a worker, who uses her head to stop the way. Their smell is also, perhaps, a protection. *Tetramorium cæspitum* has the habit of feigning death. This species, however, does not roll itself up, but merely applies its legs and antennæ closely to the body.

Formica rufa, the common horse ant, attacks in serried masses, seldom sending out detachments, while single ants scarcely ever make individual attacks. They rarely pursue a flying foe, but give no quarter, killing as many enemies as possible, and never hesitating, with this object, to sacrifice themselves for the common good.

Formica sanguinea, on the contrary, at least in their slave-making expeditions, attempt rather to terrify than to kill. Indeed, when they are invading a nest, they do not attack the flying inhabitants, unless the latter are attempting to carry off pupæ, in which case they are forced to abandon these. When fighting, they attempt to crush their enemies with their mandibles.

Formica exsecta is a delicate, but very active species. They also advance in serried masses, but in close quarters they bite right and left, dancing about to avoid being bitten themselves. When fighting with larger species, they spring on to their backs, and then seize them by the neck or by an antenna. They also have the instinct of combining in small parties, three or four seizing an enemy at once, and then pulling different ways, so that she on her part cannot get at any one of her foes. One of them then jumps on her back and cuts, or rather saws off, her head. In battles between this ant and the much larger *F. pratensis*, many of the latter may be seen, each with a little *F. exsecta* on her back, sawing off her head from behind.

One might, at first sight, be disposed to consider that the ants with stings must have a great advantage over those with none. In some cases, however, the poison is so strong that it is sufficient for it to touch the foes to place them *hors de combat*, or at least to render them incapacitated, with every appearance of extreme pain. Such species have the abdomen unusually mobile.

The species of *Lasius* make up in numbers what they want in strength. Several of them seize an enemy at the same time, one by each of her legs or antennæ, and when they have once taken hold they will suffer themselves to be cut in pieces rather than let go.

Polyergus rufescens, the celebrated slave-making or Amazon ant, has a mode of combat almost peculiar to herself. Her jaws are very powerful, and pointed. If attacked—if, for instance, another ant seizes her by a leg—she at once takes her enemy's head into her jaws, thus generally making her quit her hold. If she does not, the *Polyergus* closes her mandibles, so that the points pierce the brain of her enemy, paralyzing the nervous system. The victim falls in convulsions,

setting free her terrible foe. In this manner a comparatively small force of *Polyergus* will fearlessly
attack much larger armies of other species, suffering
itself scarcely any loss.

I have elsewhere discussed the relations of flowers
to insects, especially to bees, and particularly the
mode in which flowers have been modified, so that
the bees might transfer the pollen from one to another.
Ants are also, as mentioned in the preceding lecture,
of considerable importance to plants, especially in keeping down the number of insects which feed on them.
So far as I know, however, there are no plants which
are specially modified, in order to be fertilized by
ants; and, indeed, even to those small flowers which
any little insect might fertilize, the visits of winged
insects are much more advantageous; because, as Mr.
Darwin has shown in his excellent work on cross-
and self-fertilization of plants, it is important that
the pollen should be brought, not only from a different
flower, but also from a different plant, while creeping
insects, such as ants, would naturally pass from flower
to flower of the same plant.

Under these circumstances, it is important to plants
that ants should not obtain access to the flowers,
which they would otherwise rob of their honey, without conferring on them any compensating advantage.
Accordingly, we not only find in flowers various modes
of attracting bees, but also of excluding ants; and
in this way ants have exercised more influence on
the vegetable kingdom than might be supposed. Sometimes, for instance, flowers are protected by *chevaux
de frise* of spines and fine hairs pointing downwards

H

(*Carlina, Lamium*) ; some have a number of glands secreting a glutinous substance, over which the ants cannot pass (*Linnæa*, Gooseberry) ; in others the tube of the flower is itself very narrow, or is almost closed either by hairs or by internal ridges, which just leave space for the proboscis of a bee, but no more. Lastly, some, and especially pendulous flowers (*Cyclamen*, Snowdrop), are so smooth and slippery that ants cannot easily enter them, but often slip off in the attempt, and thus are excluded ; just as the pendulous nests of the weaver-birds preclude the entrance of snakes.

ON THE HABITS OF ANTS.

II.

Mr. Grote, in his *Fragments on Ethical Subjects*, regards it as an evident necessity that no society can exist without the sentiment of morality. " Every one," he says, " who has either spoken or written on the subject has agreed in considering this sentiment as absolutely indispensable to the very existence of society. Without the diffusion of a certain measure of this feeling throughout all the members of the social union, the caprices, the desires, and the passions of each separate individual would render the maintenance of any established communion impossible. Positive morality, under some form or other, has existed in every society of which the world has ever had experience." [1]

If this be so, then ants must be moral and accountable beings. I cannot, however, urge this myself, having elsewhere attempted to show that, even with reference to man, the case is not by any means clear.

As regards ants, various observers have recorded instances of attachment and affection. In various memoirs

[1] III. p. 497.

published by the Linnean Society, I have discussed these cases, and have reluctantly come to the conclusion that some of them, at any rate, rest on a very doubtful foundation.

Yet I am far from denying that such instances do exist. For example, in one of my nests of *Formica fusca* was a poor ant which had come into the world without antennæ. Never having previously met with such a case, I watched her with great interest, but she never appeared to leave the nest. At length one day I found her wandering about in an aimless sort of manner, and apparently not knowing her way at all. After a while she fell in with some specimens of *L. flavus*, who directly attacked her. I at once set myself to separate them, but whether owing to the wounds she had received from her enemies, or to my rough, though well-meant, handling, or to both, she was evidently sorely wounded, and lay helpless on the ground. After some time, another *F. fusca* from her nest came by. She examined the poor sufferer carefully, then picked her up tenderly and carried her away into the nest. It would have been difficult for any one who witnessed the scene to have denied to this ant the possession of humane feelings. I might quote various more or less similar cases; nevertheless they are, according to my experience, exceptional. Indeed, I have often been surprised that in certain emergencies ants render one another so little assistance. The tenacity with which they retain their hold on an enemy they have once seized is well known. M. Mocquerys even assures us that the Indians of Brazil made use of this quality in the case of wounds, causing an ant to bite the two lips of the cut and thus bring them

together, after which the Indians cut off the ant's head,
which thus holds the lips of the wound together.   He
asserts that he has often seen natives with wounds in
course of healing by the assistance of seven or eight
ants' heads ! [1]   I have often observed that some of my
ants had the heads of others hanging on to their legs
for a considerable time, and as this must certainly
be very inconvenient, it seems remarkable that their
friends should not relieve them of such an awkward
encumbrance.

As mentioned in the previous lecture, one of my
queen ants (*Formica fusca*) had a large mite on the
under side of her head.   She could not remove it, and
not one of her companions, for more than three months,
performed this kind office for her.   Being a queen, she
never left the nest, and I therefore had no opportunity
of helping her.   Since then I have met with several
similar cases.   Moreover, I have often put ants, which
had become smeared with a sticky substance, on the
boards close to my nests, and very rarely indeed did
their companions take any notice of, or seek to dis-
entangle them.

Again, if an ant be fighting with one of another
species, her friends rarely come to her assistance.   They
seem generally (unless a regular battle is taking place)
to take no interest in the matter, and do not even stop
to look on.   Some species, indeed, never in such con-
tests appear to help one another ; and even when they
do so, as, for instance, in the genus *Lasius*, the truth
seems to be that several of them attack the same enemy,

[1] *Ann. Soc. Ent. France*, 2 Sér. tom. ii. p. 67.

—their object being to destroy the foe, not to save their friend.

To test the affection of ants for one another, I have made a number of experiments, from which I will extract a few, as specimens of the whole. Thus, January 3, 1876, I immersed an ant (*F. nigra*) in water for half an hour, and when she was then, to all appearance, drowned, I put her on a strip of paper, leading to some food. The strip was half an inch wide, and one of my marked ants belonging to the same nest was passing continually to and fro over it. The immersed ant lay there an hour before she recovered herself, and during this time the marked ant passed by eighteen times without taking the slightest notice of her.

I then immersed another ant in water for an hour, after which I placed her on the strip of paper, as in the preceding case. She was three-quarters of an hour before she recovered ; during this time two marked ants were passing to and fro ; one of them went by eighteen times, the other twenty times, two other ants also went over the paper, but none of them took the slightest notice of their half-drowned friend.

As evidence both of their intelligence and of their affection for their friends, it has been said by various observers that when ants have been accidentally buried, they have been very soon dug out and rescued by their companions. Without for a moment doubting the facts as stated, we must remember the habit which ants have of burrowing in loose fresh soil, and especially their practice of digging out fresh galleries, when their nests are disturbed. It seemed to me, however, that it would not be difficult to test whether the excavations made by ants

under the circumstances were the result of this general
habit, or really due to a desire to extricate their friends.
With this view, I tried (20th August) the following
experiments. I placed some honey near a nest of *Lasius
niger* on a glass surrounded with water, and so arranged
that in reaching it the ants passed over another glass
covered with a layer of sifted earth about one-third of
an inch in thickness. I then put some ants to the
honey, and by degrees a considerable number collected
round it. Then at 1.30 P.M., I buried an ant from the
same nest under the earth, and left her there till 5 P.M.,
when I uncovered her. She was none the worse, but
during the whole time, not one of her friends had taken
the least notice of her.

Again, September 1st, I arranged some honey in the
same way. At 5 P.M. about fifty ants were at the honey,
and a considerable number were passing to and fro. I
then buried an ant as before, of course taking one from
the same nest. At 7 P.M. the number of ants at the
honey had nearly doubled. At 10 P.M. they were still
more numerous, and had carried off about two-thirds of
the honey. At 7 A.M. the next morning the honey was
all gone; two or three ants were still wandering about,
but no notice had been taken of the prisoner, whom I
then let out. In this case I allowed the honey to be
finished, because I thought it might perhaps be alleged
that the excitement produced by such a treasure dis-
tracted their attention; or even, on the principle
of doing the greatest good to the greatest number,
that they were intelligently wise in securing a treasure of food before they rescued their comrade, who,
though in confinement, was neither in pain nor danger,

So far as the above ants, however, are concerned, this cannot be urged. I may add that I repeated the same experiment several times, in some cases with another species, *Myrmica ruginodis*, and always with the same results.

I then tried the following experiment. A number of the small yellow ants (*L. flavus*) were out feeding on some honey. I took five of them, and also five others of the same species, but from a different nest, chloroformed them, and put them close to the honey, and on the path which the ants took in going to and from the nest, so that these could not but see them. The glass on which the honey was placed was surrounded by a moat of water. This, I thought, would give me an opportunity of testing both how far they would be disposed to assist a fellow-creature, and what difference they would make between their nest companions and strangers from a different community of the same species. The chloroformed ants were put down at 10 in the morning. For more than an hour, though many ants came up and touched them with their antennæ, none did more. At length one of the strangers was picked up, carried to the edge of the glass, and quietly thrown, or rather dropped, into the water. Shortly afterwards a friend was taken up and treated in the same way. By degrees they were all picked up and thrown into the water. One of the strangers was, indeed, taken into the nest, but in about half an hour she was brought out again and thrown into the water like the rest. I repeated this experiment with fifty ants, half friends and half strangers. In each case twenty out of the twenty-five ants were thrown into the water as described. A few were left lying where they were placed, and these also, if we had watched longer, would no doubt have been also treated in the same way. One out of the twenty-five friends, and three out of the twenty-five strangers, were carried into the nest, but they were all brought out again, and thrown away like the rest. Under such circumstances, then, it seems that ants make no difference between friends and strangers.

It may, however, be said, as to this experiment, that since ants do not recover from chloroform, and these ants were therefore to all intents and purposes dead, we should not expect that much difference would be made between friends and strangers. I therefore tried the same experiment again, only, instead of chloroforming the ants, I made them intoxicated. This was rather more difficult. No ant would voluntarily degrade herself by getting drunk, and it was not easy in all cases to hit off the requisite degree of this compulsory intoxication. In all cases they were made quite drunk, so that they lay helplessly on their backs. The sober ants seemed much puzzled at finding their friends in this helpless and discreditable condition. They took them up and carried them about for a while in a sort of aimless way, as if they did not know what to do with their drunkards, any more than we do. Ultimately, however, the results were as follows. The ants removed twenty-five friends and thirty strangers. Of the friends twenty were carried into the nest, where no doubt they slept off the effect of the spirit—at least we saw no more of them— and five were thrown into the water. Of the strangers, on the contrary, twenty-four were thrown into the water; only six were taken into the nest, and four at least of these were afterwards brought out again and thrown away.

The difference in the treatment of friends and strangers was therefore most marked. Dead ants, I may add, are always brought out of the nest, and I have more than once found a little heap on one spot, giving it all the appearance of a burial-ground.

Again I tried the following experiment. I took six ants from a nest of *Formica fusca*, and imprisoned them in a small bottle, one end of which was left open, but covered by a layer of muslin. I then put the bottle close to the door of the nest. The muslin was of open texture, the meshes, however, being sufficiently small to prevent the ants from escaping. They could not only, however, see one another, but communicate freely with their antennæ. We now watched to see whether the prisoners would be tended or fed by their friends. We could not, however, observe that the least notice was taken of them. The experiment, nevertheless; was less conclusive than could be wished, because they might have been fed at night, or at some time when we were not looking. It struck me, therefore, that it would be interesting to treat some strangers also in the same manner.

On September 2, therefore, I put two ants from one of my nests of *F. fusca* into a bottle, the end of which was tied up with muslin as described, and laid it down close to the nest. In a second bottle I put two ants from another nest of the same species. The ants which were at liberty took no notice of the bottle containing their imprisoned friends. The strangers in the other bottle, on the contrary, excited them considerably. The whole day one, two, or more ants stood sentry, as it were, over the bottle, in a state of considerable excitement.

By the evening, no less than twelve were collected round it, a larger number than usually came out of the nest at any one time. The whole of the next two days, in the same way, there were more or less ants round the bottle containing the strangers; while, as far as we could see, no notice whatever was taken of the friends. Eventually the ants succeeded in biting through the muslin and effecting an entrance, when they attacked the strangers. On the other hand, the friends were throughout quite neglected.

Sept. 21.—I then repeated the experiment, putting three ants from another nest in a bottle as before. The same scene was repeated. The friends were neglected. On the other hand, some of the ants were always watching over the bottle containing the strangers, and biting at the muslin which protected them. The next morning, at 6 A.M., I found five ants thus occupied. One had caught hold of the leg of one of the strangers, which had unwarily been allowed to protrude through the meshes of the muslin. They worked and watched, though not, as far as I could see, upon any system, till 7.30 in the evening, when they effected an entrance, and immediately attacked the strangers.

Sept. 24.—I repeated the same experiment with the same nest. Again the ants came and sat over the bottle containing the strangers, while no notice was taken of the friends.

The next morning, again, when I got up, I found five ants round the bottle containing the strangers, none near the friends. As in the former case, one of the ants had seized a stranger by the leg, and was trying to drag her through the muslin. All day the ants clustered round

the bottle, and bit perseveringly, though not system-
atically, at the muslin.   The same thing happened also
on the following day.

These observations seemed to me sufficiently to test
the behaviour of the ants belonging to this nest, under
these circumstances.   I thought it desirable, however, to
try also other communities.   I selected, therefore, two
other nests.   One was a community of *Polyergus rufescens* with numerous slaves.   Close to where the ants of
this nest came to feed, I placed, as before, two small
bottles closed in the   same way—one containing two
slave ants from the   nest, the other two   strangers.
These ants, however, behaved quite unlike the preceding,
for they took no notice of either bottle, and showed no
sign either of affection or hatred.   One is almost tempted
to surmise that the warlike spirit of these ants was
broken by slavery.

The other nest which I tried, also a community of
Formica fusca, behaved exactly like the first.   They
took no notice of the bottle containing the friends, but
clustered round, and eventually forced their way into,
that containing the strangers.

It seems, therefore, that in these curious insects hatred
is a stronger passion than affection.

Moreover, as regards the affection of bees for one
another, it is no doubt true that when they have got any
honey on them they are always licked clean by the
others, but I am satisfied that this is more for the
sake of the honey than of the bee.   I have, for instance, several times experimented with two bees; one
of which had been drowned, while the other was smeared
with honey.   The latter was soon licked clean; of the

former no notice whatever was taken. I have, moreover, repeatedly placed dead bees close to honey on which live ones were feeding, but the latter never took the slightest notice of the corpses.

It is clear from the experiments recorded in the present and in my last lecture, that ants recognize all their fellows in the same nest, but it is very difficult to understand how this can be effected. The nests vary very much in size, but in several species 100,000 individuals may probably be by no means an unusual number, and in some instances even this is largely exceeded. Now it seems almost incredible that in such nests every ant should know every other one by sight.

It has been suggested, in the case of bees, that each nest might have some sign or password.

The whole subject is full of difficulty. It occurred to me, however, that experiments with pupæ might throw some light upon it. Although the ants of different nests are generally deadly enemies, still, if larvæ or pupæ from one nest are transferred to another of the same species, they are kindly received, and tended with apparently as much care as if they really belonged to the nest. In ant warfare, though sex is no protection, the young are spared—at least when they belong to the same species. Moreover, though the habits and disposition of ants are greatly changed if they are taken away from their nest and kept in solitary confinement, or only with a few friends, still under such circumstances they will carefully tend any young which may be confided to them. Now, if the recognition were effected by means of some signal or password, then, as it can hardly be supposed that the larvæ or pupæ would be sufficiently intelligent to appreciate, still less to remember it, the pupæ which were entrusted to ants from another nest would have the password, if any, of that nest : and not of the one from which they had been taken. Hence, if the recognition were effected by some password, or sign with the antennæ, they would be amicably received in the nest from which their nurses had been taken, but not in their own. . I therefore took a number of pupæ out of some of my nests of *Formica fusca* and *Lasius niger*, and put them in small glasses, some with ants from their own nest, some with ants from another nest of the same species. The result of my observations was that thirty-two ants belonging to *Formica fusca* and *Lasius niger*, removed from their own nest as pupæ, attended by friends, and restored to their own nest, were all amicably received.

What is still more remarkable : of twenty-two ants belonging to *Formica fusca*, removed as pupæ, attended by strangers, and returned to their own nest, twenty were amicably received, though in several cases after some hesitation. As regards one, I was doubtful : this last was crippled in coming out of the pupa case, and to this perhaps her unfriendly reception may have been due. Of the same number of *Lasius niger*, developed in the same manner, from pupæ tended by strangers belonging to the same species, and then returned into their own nest, seventeen were amicably received, three were attacked, and about two I felt doubtful.

On the other hand, fifteen specimens, belonging to the same species, removed as pupæ, tended by strangers belonging to the same species, and then put into the strangers' nest, were all attacked.

The results may be tabulated as follows :

Pupæ brought up by friends and replaced in their own nest.	Pupæ brought up by strangers.	
	Put in own nest.	Put in strangers nest.
Attacked . . . 0	7[1]	15
Received amicably 33	37	0

I hope to make further experiments in this direction, but the above results seem very interesting. They appear to indicate that ants of the same nest do not recognize one another by any password. On the other hand, if ants are removed from a nest in the pupa state, tended by strangers, and then restored, some at least of their relatives are certainly puzzled, and, in many cases, doubt their claim to consanguinity. Strangers, under the same circumstances, would be immediately attacked ; these ants, on the contrary, were in most cases—sometimes, however, only after examination—amicably received by the majority of the colony, and it was often several hours before they came across a single individual who did not recognize them.

Most of our European ants feed on honey, or on other insects. Some few, however, store up grain.

A Texan ant, *Pogonomyrmex barbatus*, is also a harvesting species, storing up especially the grains of *Aristida oligantha*, the so-called " ant rice," and of a grass, *Buchlœ dactyloides*. These ants clear disks, ten or twelve feet in diameter, round the entrance to their nest, a work of no small labour in the rich soil, and under the hot sun, of Texas. I say clear a disk, but some, though not all, of these disks are occupied, especially round the edge, by a growth of ant rice.

---

[1] About three of these I did not feel sure.

Dr. Lincecum, who first gave an account of these insects, maintained not only that the ground was carefully cleared of all other plants, but that this grass was intentionally cultivated by the ants. Mr. McCook, by whom the subject has been recently studied, fully confirms Dr. Lincecum that the disks are kept carefully clean, that the ant rice alone is permitted to grow on them, and ꙮhat the produce of this crop is carefully harvested ; but he thinks that the ant rice sows itself, and is not actually planted by the ants.

Much of what has been said as to the powers of communication possessed by bees and ants depends on the fact that if one of them in the course of her rambles has discovered a supply of food, a number of others soon find their way to the store. This, however, does not necessarily imply any power of describing localities. If the bees or ants merely follow a more fortunate companion, or if they hunt her by scent, the matter is comparatively simple ; if, on the contrary, the others have the route described to them, the case becomes very different. To determine this, therefore, I have made a great number of experiments, of which, however, I will here only mention a few. Under ordinary circumstances, if an ant discovers a stock of food, she carries as much as possible away to the nest, and then returns for more, accompanied generally by several friends. On their return these bring others, and in this way a string of ants is soon established. Unless, therefore, various precautions are taken, and this, so far as I know, has never been done in any previous observations, the experiment really tells very little.

The following may be taken as a type of what happens

under such circumstances.　On June 12, I put a *Lasius niger*, belonging to a nest which I had kept two or three days without food, to some honey.　She fed as usual, and then was returning to the nest, when she met some friends, whom she proceeded to feed.　When she had thus distributed her stores, she returned alone to the honey, none of the rest coming with her.　When she had a second time laid in a stock of food, she again in the same way fed several ants on her way towards the nest ; but this time five of those so fed returned with her to the honey.　In due course these five would no doubt have brought others, and so the number at the honey would have increased.

Some species, however, act much more in association than others—*Lasius niger*, for instance, much more than *Formica fusca*.　I have already given an illustration of what happens when a *Lasius niger* finds a store of food.　The following is a great contrast.　On the 28th March, I was staying at Arcachon.　It was a beautiful and very warm spring day, and numerous ants were coursing about on the flagstones in front of our hotel.

At about 10.45 I put a *Formica fusca* to a raisin. She fed till 11.2, when she went almost straight to her nest, which was about 12 feet away.　In a few minutes she came out again, and returned to the fruit, after a few small wanderings, at about 11.18.　She then fed till 11.30, when she returned to the nest.

At 11.45 another ant accidentally found the fruit.　I imprisoned her.

At 11.50 the first returned, and fed till 11.56, when she went off to the nest.　On the way she met and talked with three ants, none of whom, however, came to the raisin. At 12.7 she returned, again alone, to the fruit.

On the following day I repeated the same experiment. There were perhaps even more ants about than on the previous day.

At 9.45 I put one (N 1) to a raisin.   At 9.50 she went to the nest.

9.55 I put another (N 2) to the raisin.	10.0 ,,
10.0 N 1 came back.	10.2 ,,
10.7 ,, ,,	10.9 ,,
10.11 N 2 ,,	10.13 ,,
10.12 N 1 ,,	10.14 ,,
10.13 put another (N 3) to the raisin.	10.18 ,,
10.16 N 1 back.	10.17 ,,
10.22 N 2 ,,	10.24 ,,

(N 2 met with an accident and returned no more.) [nest.

10.24 N 1 back.	At 10.26 went to the
10.30 N 1 ,,	10.32 ,,
10.33 N 3 ,,	10.35 ,,

10.35 N 1   ,,   (She met with an accident. At first she seemed a good deal hurt, but gradually recovered.)

10.40 N 3 back.	At 10.46 she went to
10.46 a stranger came; I imprisoned her.	[the nest.
10.47 ,, ,, ,,	
10.52 N 1 back.	10.54 ,,
10.57 N 3 ,,	11.2 ,,
11.8 N 3 ,,	11.13 ,,

11.10 a stranger came; I removed her to a little distance.

11.11   ,,   ,,   marked her N 4.

11.16 N 3 back.	At 11.18 went.
11.23 N 4 ,,	11.25 ,,
11.24 N 3 ,,	11.26 ,,
11.27 N 4 ,,	11.29 ,,
11.31 N 3 ,,	11.34 ,,
11.32 N 4 ,,	11.35 ,,
11.40 N 3 ,,	11.42 ,,
11.40 N 4 ,,	11.42 ,,
11.45 N 3 ,,	11.47 ,,

11.45 a stranger came.

At 11.48 N 1 came.   At 11.49 went.
   11.49 N 4   „   11.50   „
   11.51 N 1   „   11.53   „
   11.53 N 3   „   11.56   „
   11.54 N 4   „   11.56   „
   12.0 N 3   „   12.2   „
   12.0 N 4   „   12.2   „
   12.0 N 1   „   12.2   „
   12.5 N 4   „   12.7   „
   12.6 N 3   „   12.8   „
   12.13 N 3   „   12.15   „
   12.14 N 4   „   12.15   „
   12.17 a stranger came.
   12.19 N 4 came.   12.20   „
   12.20 N 3   „   12.22   „
   12.21 N 1   „   12.25   „
   12.25 N 4   „   12.26   „
   12.27 N 3   „   12.28   „
   12.30 N 4   „   12.32   „
   12.30 a stranger came.
   12.30 N 3 (was disturbed)   12.37   „
   12.38 N 4 came.   12.40   „
   12.42 N 3   „
   12.47 N 4   „   12.49   „

Thus, during these three hours only six strangers came. The raisin must have seemed almost inexhaustible, and the watched ants in passing and repassing went close to many of their friends ; these took no notice of them, however, and did not bring any out of the nest to co-operate with them in securing the food, though their regular visits showed how much they appreciated it.

Again (on the 15th July) an ant belonging to one of my nests of *Formica fusca* was out hunting. At 8.8, I put a spoonful of honey before her. She fed till 8.24, when she returned to the nest. Several others were running about. She returned regularly at short intervals, but during the whole day she brought no friend, and only one other ant found the honey, evidently an independent discovery.

The species of *Lasius*, as already mentioned, behave very differently. To determine, if possible, whether they can send, as well as bring, their friends to stores of food, I made a number of experiments. For instance, one of my nests of the small brown garden ant, *Lasius niger*, was connected with a board, on which I was in the habit of placing a supply of food and water. At a short distance from the board I placed two glasses (Fig. 49 b b'), and on b I placed some food. I then connected the glass b with the board a by three slips of paper, c, d, e, and put an ant to the food. She carried off a supply to the nest, returning for more, and so on. Several friends came with her, and I imprisoned them till the experiment was over. When she had passed several times over the paper bridges, I proceeded as follows. Any friends who came with her were excluded from the bridges when she was on them. If she was not there, as soon as a friend arrived at the bridge c, I took up the paper e in my fingers and rubbed it lightly, with a view of removing or blurring the scent; and as soon as the ant arrived on d, I took up the bridge c, and put it across the chasm from d to b. Now, if the ant acted on information received, she would of course cross e to b. If, on the other hand, she went by scent, then she would be at least as likely to go over c to b'. The result was, that out of about one hundred and twenty friends who passed over d, only twenty went to the food; while nearly one hundred passed over c to the empty glass. In this case, the friends generally came more or less in sight of one another to the bridge c, and once there, could hardly avoid arriving either at b or b'. I therefore modified the experiment as follows. I established and endowed an ant as before, imprisoning the friends who came with her. When she knew her way thoroughly, I allowed her to return to the nest on her own legs, but as soon as she emerged again I took her up on a slip of paper, and transferred her to the food.

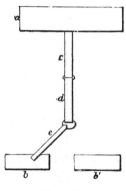

FIG. 49.

Under these circumstances, as will be seen, very few ants indeed ever found their way to the food. I began at 5.30, at which time the ant returned to the nest. At 5.34 she came out with no less than ten friends, and was then transferred to the food. The others wandered about a little, but by degrees returned to the nest, not one of them finding her way to the food. The first ant took some food, returned, and again came out of the nest at 5.39 with eight friends, when exactly the same happened. She again came out

At 5.44 with 4 friends.	At 6.44 with 0 friends.
„ 5.47 „ 4 „	„ 6.46 „ 3 „
„ 5.49 „ 1 „	„ 6.49 „ 2 „
„ 5.52	„ 6.56
„ 5.54 „ 5 „	„ 6.59
„ 5.58 „ 2 „	„ 7.2 „ 2 „
„ 5.59 „ 2 „	„ 7.4
„ 6.1 „ 5 „	„ 7.6 „ 3 „
„ 6.4 „ 1 „	„ 7.8 „ 3 „
„ 6.7	„ 7.10 „ 5 „
„ 6.11 „ 3 „	„ 7.13
„ 6.14 „ 4 „	„ 7.17 „ 3 „
„ 6.17 „ 6 „	„ 7.19 „ 7 „
„ 6.20	„ 7.21 „ 5 „
„ 6.23 „ 5 „	„ 7.24
„ 6.25 „ 6 „	„ 7.26 „ 3 „
„ 6.29 „ 8 „	„ 7.29 „ 1 „
„ 6.32 „ 2 „	„ 7.31 „ 2 „
„ 6.35	„ 7.35
„ 6.42 „ 4 „	

(39 journeys ; 11 alone, 28 with 120 friends.)

Thus, during these two hours, more than one hundred and twenty ants came out of the nest, in company with the one under observation. She knew her way perfectly, and it is clear that, if she had been let alone, all these ants would have accompanied her to the store of food. Three of them were accidentally allowed to do so, but of the remainder only five found their way to the food ; all the others, after wandering about a while, returned empty-handed to the nest.

I conclude, then, that when large numbers of ants come to food they follow one another, being also to a certain extent guided by scent. The fact, therefore, does not imply any considerable power of intercommunication. There are, moreover, some circumstances which seem to point in an opposite direction.   For instance, I have already mentioned that, if a colony of the slave-making ant changes the situation of its nest, the mistresses are all carried to the new nest by the slaves.   Again, if a number of *F. fusca* are put in a box, and if in one corner a dark place of retreat be provided for them, with some earth, one soon finds her way to it.   She then comes out again, and going up to one of the others, takes her by the jaws.   The second ant then rolls herself into a heap, and is carried off to the place of shelter.   They then both repeat the same manœuvre with other ants, and so on until all their companions are collected toge-ther.   Now it seems to me difficult to imagine that so slow a course would be adopted, if they possessed any power of communicating description.

On the other hand, they certainly can, I think, trans-mit simpler ideas.   In support of this, I may adduce the following experiment.   Two strips of paper were attached to the board just mentioned (p. 116), parallel to one another; and at the other end of each I placed a piece of glass.   In the glass, at the end of one tape, I placed a considerable number (three to six hundred) of larvæ. In the second I put two or three larvæ only.   I then took two ants, and placed one of them to the glass with many larvæ, the other to that with two or three.   Each of them took a larva and carried it to the nest, return-ing for another, and so on.   After each journey I put another larva in the glass with only two or three larvæ, to replace that which had been removed.   Now, if other ants came, under the above circumstances, as a mere matter of accident, or accompanying one another by chance, or if they simply saw the larvæ which were being brought, and consequently concluded that they might themselves also find larvæ in the same place, then the numbers going to the two glasses ought to be approximately equal. In each case the number of journeys made by the ants would be nearly the same; consequently, if it were a matter of smell, the two routes would be in the same condition. It would be impossible for an ant, seeing another in the act of bringing a larva, to judge for herself whether there were few or many larvæ left behind. On the other hand, if the strangers were brought, then it would be curious to see whether more were brought to the glass with many larvæ than to that which only contained two or three. I should mention that every stranger was imprisoned, until the end of the experiment. I select a few of the results :—

Exp. 1. Time occupied, one hour. The ant with few larvæ made 6 visits, and brought no friends. The one with many larvæ made 7, and brought 11 friends.

Exp. 3. Time occupied, three hours. The ant with few larvæ made 24 journeys, and brought 5 friends. The one with many larvæ made 38 journeys, and brought 22 friends.

Exp. 5. Time occupied, one hour. The ant with few larvæ made 10 journeys, and brought 3 friends. The other made 5 journeys, and brought 16 friends.

Exp. 9. Time occupied, one hour. The ant with few larvæ made 11 journeys, and brought 1 friend. The one with many larvæ made 15 journeys, and brought 13 friends.

Exp. 10. I now reversed the glasses, the same two ants being under observation; but the ant which in the previous observation had few larvæ to carry off now consequently had many, and *vice versâ*.   Time occupied, two hours.   The ant with few larvæ made 21 journeys, and brought 1 friend.   The one with many larvæ made 22 journeys, and brought 20 friends.   These two experiments are, I think, especially striking.

Taken as a whole, I found that in about fifty hours, the ants which had access to many larvæ brought 257 friends, while those visiting the glass with few larvæ only brought 82.   This result will appear still more striking, if we remember that a certain number, say perhaps 25, would have come to the larvæ anyhow, which would make the numbers 232, as against 57 ; a very large difference.

Experiments with bees and wasps have led me to very similar results.   As regards wasps, a typical case has been already given (*ante*, p. 11).   In the case of bees, I have generally found that when they first discover a treasure of food, they bring a few friends with them, who in their turn are accompanied by others ; and so on.   If, however, for the first few hours of the experiment, the friends thus brought are driven away or imprisoned, other bees soon cease to come.[1]   For instance, one bee which I watched for five days during this period only brought half a dozen friends.   In my first experiments, however, the quantity of honey used was but small ; I thought, therefore, that it would be well to repeat them with a larger quantity.   Accordingly, on the 19th July, I put a bee (No. 10) to a honeycomb containing 12 lbs. of honey

---

[1] My experiments were made at an upper window.   If they had been made on the ground floor the results might have been different.

		At 12.36 she went back to the hive.
At 12.30		
„ 12.50 she returns ;	„ 12.55	„ „
„ 1.6 „	„ 1.12	„ „
„ 1.53 „	„ 1.57	„ „
„ 2.5 „	„ 2.9	„ „
„ 2.16 „	„ 2.20	„ „
„ 2.28 „	„ 2.32 ?	„ „
„ 2.49 „	„ 2.55	„ „
„ 3.13 „	„ 3.20	, · „
„ 3.31 „	„ 3.39	„ „
„ 3.45 „	„ 3.55	„ „
„ 4.2 „	„ 4.8	„ „
„ 4.18 „	„ 4.24	„ „
„ 4.31 „	„ 4.37	„ „
„ 4.47 „	„ 4.58	„ „
„ 5.10 „	„ 5.19	„ „
„ 5.27 „	„ 5.30	„ „
„ 6.9 „	„ 6.15	„ „
„ 6.23 „	„ 6.29	„ „
„ 7.19 „	„ 7.24	„ „
„ 7.35 „	„ 7.40	„ „
„ 7.50 „	„ 7.55	„ „

And during all this time no other bee came to the comb.

On the following morning, July 20th, this bee (No. 10) came to the honeycomb at 6 in the morning, and we watched her till 2 P.M. ; but during the whole of this time no other bee had come to the comb.

Bees seem also to be less clever in finding their way about than might have been expected. In some cases, indeed, flies are more intelligent. Thus, I put a bee into a bell glass 18 inches long and a mouth $6\frac{1}{2}$ inches wide, turning the closed end to the window ; she buzzed about till 11.15, when, as there seemed no chance of her getting out, I put her back into the hive. Two flies, on the contrary, which I put in with her, got out at once. At 11.30 I put another bee and a fly into the same glass ;

the latter flew out at once. For half an hour the bee tried to get out at the closed end ; I then turned the glass with its open end to the light, when she flew out at once. To make sure, I repeated the experiment once more, with the same result.

Some bees, however, have seemed to me more intelligent in this respect than others. A bee which I had fed several times, and which had flown about in the room, found its way out of the glass in a quarter of an hour, and when put in a second time, came out at once. Another bee, when I closed the postern door, used to come round to the honey through an open window.

In the previous lecture, I have mentioned that I was never able to satisfy myself that ants heard any sounds which I could produce. I would not, however, by any means infer from this that they are incapable of hearing.

Micromegas indeed concluded that as he heard no sound, men did not speak ; indeed, he asks how is it possible that such infinitesimal atoms should have organs of voice ? and what could they have to say ? Moreover, he continues, to speak it is necessary to think, or nearly so : now, to think requires a mind, and to attribute a mind to these little creatures would be absurd. We must be careful not to fall into a similar series of errors.

It is far from improbable that ants may produce sounds entirely beyond our range of hearing. Indeed, it is not impossible that insects may possess a sense, or rather perhaps sensations, of which we can no more form an idea, than we should have been able to conceive red or green, if the human race had been blind. Helmholtz and Depretz have shown that the human ear is sensitive to vibrations reaching to 38,000 in a second. The sensation of red is produced when 470 millions of millions of vibrations of ether enter the eye in a similar time; but between 38,000 and 470 millions of millions, vibrations produce on us the sensation of heat only. We have no special organs of sense adapted to them, but there is no reason in the nature of things why this should be the case with other animals, and the problematical organs possessed by many of the lower forms favour the suggestion. If any apparatus could be devised by which the number of vibrations produced by any given cause could be lowered so as to be brought within the range of our ears, it is probable that the result would be most interesting.

I have tried unsuccessfully various experiments in order to ascertain whether the ants themselves produced any sounds for the purpose of conveying signs or ideas. Professor Tyndall was so good as to arrange for me one of his sensitive flames, but I could not perceive that it responded in any way to my ants. The experiment was not, however, very satisfactory, as I was not able to try the flame with a very active nest. Professor Bell was also kind enough to set up for me an extremely sensitive microphone: it was attached to the under side of one of my nests, and though we could distinctly hear the ants walking about, we could not distinguish any other sound.

It is, however, of course possible, as I have already suggested, that ants may be sensitive to, and also themselves produce, sounds which, from the rapidity of their vibrations, or some other cause, are beyond our range of hearing. Having failed therefore in hearing them or making them hear me, I endeavoured to ascertain whether they could hear one another.

To ascertain if possible whether ants have the power of summoning one another by sound, I tried the following experiments. I put out on the board where one of my nests of *Lasius flavus* was usually fed, six small pillars of wood about an inch and a half high, and on one of them I put some honey. A number of ants were wandering about on the board itself in search of food, and the nest itself was immediately above, and about 12 inches from the board. I then put three ants to the honey, and when each had sufficiently fed I imprisoned her and put another; thus always keeping three ants at the honey, but not allowing them to go home. If then they could summon their friends by sound, there ought soon to be many ants at the honey. The results were as follows :—

Sebtember 8th.—Began at 11 A.M. Up to 3 o'clock only seven ants found their way to the honey, while about as many ran up the other pillars. The arrival of these seven, therefore, was not more than would naturally result from the numbers running about close by. At 3, I allowed the ants then on the honey to return home. The result was that from 3.6, when the first went home, to 3.30, eleven came ; from 3.30 to 4, no less than forty-three. Thus in four hours only seven came, while it was obvious that many would have wished to come if they had known about the honey, because in the next three-quarters of an hour, when they were informed of it, fifty-four came.

On the 10th September I tried the same again, keeping as before three ants on the honey, but not allowing any to go home. From 12 to 5.30, only eight came. They were then allowed to take the news. From 5.30 to 6, four came; from 6 to 6.30, four; from 6.30 to 7, eight; from 7.30 to 8, no less than fifty-one.

Again, on September 30th, I tried the same arrangement, again beginning at 11. Up to 3.30, seven ants came. We then let them go. From 3.30 to 4.30, twenty-eight came. From 4.30 to 5, fifty-one came. Thus in four hours and a half only seven came; while, when they were allowed to return, no less than seventy-nine came in an hour and a half. It seems obvious therefore that in these cases no communication was transmitted by sound.

In order further to test how far ants are guided by sight and how much by scent, I tried the following experiment with *Lasius niger*. Some food was put out at

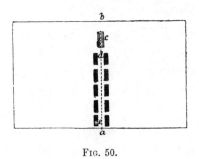

Fig. 50.

the point *a* on a board measuring 20 inches by 12 (Fig. 50), and so arranged that the ants in going straight to it from the nest would reach the board at the point *b*, and after passing under a paper tunnel, *c*, would proceed between five pairs of wooden bricks, each three inches in length and 1¾ in height. When they got to know their

way, they went quite straight along the line *d e* to *a*.
The board was then twisted as shown in Fig. 51. The

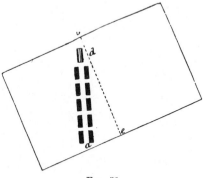

FIG. 51.

bricks and tunnel being arranged exactly in the same
direction as before, but the board having been moved,
the line *d e* was now outside them. This change, however, did not at all discompose the ants; but instead of
going, as before, through the tunnel and between the

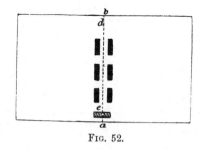

FIG. 52.

rows of bricks to *a*, they walked exactly along the old
path to *e*.

I then arranged matters as before, but without the
tunnel and with only three pairs of bricks (Fig. 52).
When an ant had got quite used to the path *d* to *e*, I

altered the position of the bricks and food to f (Fig. 53),
making a difference of 8 inches in the position of the

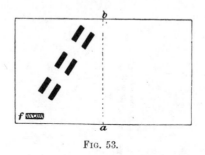

FIG. 53.

latter. The ant came as before, walked up to the first
brick, touched it with her antennæ, but then followed her
old line to a. From there she veered towards the food,
and very soon found it. When she was gone, I altered
it again, as shown in Fig. 54 ; she returned after the usual

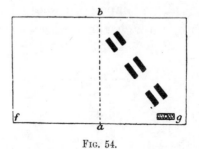

FIG. 54.

interval, and went again straight to a ; then, after some
wanderings, to f, and at length, but only after a lapse
of 25 minutes, found the food at g. These experiments
were repeated more than once, and always with similar
results. I then varied matters by removing the bricks ;
this, however, did not seem to make any difference
to the ants.

From the observations of Sprengel, there could of

course be little, if any, doubt, that bees are capable of distinguishing colours; but I have in my previous papers, read before the Linnean Society, recorded some experiments which put the matter beyond a doubt. Under these circumstances, I have been naturally anxious to ascertain, if possible, whether the same is the case with ants. I have, however, found more difficulty in doing so, because, as shown in the observations just recorded, ants find their food so much more by smell than by sight.

I tried, for instance, placing food at the bottom of a pillar of coloured paper, and then moving both the pillar and the food. The pillar, however, did not seem to help the ant (*Lasius niger*) at all to find her way to the food. I then, as recorded in my previous paper, placed the food on the top of a rod of wood 8 inches high, and when the ant knew her way perfectly well to the food, so that she went quite straight backwards and forwards to the nest, I found that if I moved the pillar of wood only 6 inches, the ant was quite bewildered, and wandered about backwards and forwards, round and round, and at last only found the pillar, as it were, accidentally.

Therefore, I could not apply to ants those tests which had been used in the case of bees. At length, however, it occurred to me that I might utilize the dislike which ants, when in their nests, have to light. Of course they have no such feeling when they are out in search of food; but if light be let in upon their nests, they at once hurry about in search of the darkest corners, and there they all congregate. If, for instance, I uncovered one of my nests and then placed an opaque

K

substance over one portion, the ants invariably collected in the shaded part.

I therefore procured four similar strips of glass, coloured respectively green, yellow, red, and blue, or rather, violet.   The yellow was rather paler in shade, and that glass consequently rather more transparent than the red or violet.   I then laid the strips of glass on one of my nests of *Formica fusca*, containing about 170 ants. These ants, as I knew by many previous observations, seek darkness, and would certainly collect under any opaque substance.

I then, after counting the ants under each strip, moved the colours gradually at intervals of about half an hour, so that each should by turns cover the same portion of the nest.   The results were as follows, the numbers indicating the approximate number of ants under each glass (there were sometimes a few not under any of the strips of glass) :—

1 . . .	Green.	Yellow.	Red.	Violet.
	50	40	80	0
2 . . .	Violet.	Green.	Yellow.	Red.
	0	20	40	100
3 . . .	Red.	Violet.	Green.	Yellow.
	60	0	50	50
4 . . .	Yellow.	Red.	Violet.	Green.
	50	70	1	40
5 . . .	Green.	Yellow.	Red.	Violet.
	30	30	100	0
6 . . .	Violet.	Green.	Yellow.	Red.
	0	14	5	140
7 . . .	Red.	Violet.	Green.	Yellow.
	50	0	40	70
8 . . .	Yellow.	Red.	Violet.	Green.
	40	50	1	70
9 . . .	Green.	Yellow.	Red.	Violet.
	60	35	65	0

10 . . .	Violet.	Green.	Yellow.	Red.
	1	50	40	70
11 . . .	Red.	Violet.	Green.	Yellow.
	50	2	50	60
12 . . .	Yellow.	Red.	Violet.	Green.
	35	55	0	70

Adding these numbers together, there were, in the twelve observations, under the red 890, under the green 544, under the yellow 495, and under the violet only 5. The difference between the red and the green is very striking, and would doubtless have been more so, but for the fact, that when the colours were transposed, the ants which had collected under the red sometimes remained quiet, as, for instance, in cases 7 and 8.

The case of the violet glass is more marked and more interesting. To our eyes, the violet was as opaque as the red, more so than the green, and much more so than the yellow. Yet, as the numbers show, the ants had scarcely any tendency to congregate under it. There were nearly as many under the same area of the uncovered portion of the nest as under that shaded by the violet glass.

Lasius flavus also showed a marked avoidance of the violet glass.

I then experimented in the same way with a nest of *Formica fusca*, in which there were some pupæ, which were generally collected in a single heap. I used glasses coloured dark yellow, dark green, light yellow, light green, red, violet, and dark purple. The colours were always in the preceding order, but, as before, their place over the nest was changed after every observation.

To our eyes, the purple was almost black, the violet and dark green very dark and quite opaque; the pupæ could be dimly seen through the red, rather more clearly through the dark yellow and light green, while the light yellow were almost transparent. There were about 50 pupæ, and the light was the ordinary diffused daylight of summer.

These observations showed a marked preference for the greens and yellows. The pupæ were $6\frac{1}{2}$ times under dark green, 3 under dark yellow, $3\frac{1}{2}$ under red, and once each under light yellow and light green, the violet and purple being altogether neglected.

I now tried the same ants under the same colours, only in the sun; and placed a shallow dish containing some 10 per cent. solution of alum, sometimes over the yellow, sometimes over the red. I also put four thicknesses of violet glass, so that it looked almost black.

Under these circumstances, the pupæ were placed under the red $7\frac{1}{2}$ times, dark yellow $5\frac{1}{2}$, and never under the violet, purple, light yellow, dark or light green.

The following day I placed, over the same nest, in the sun, dark green glass, dark red and dark yellow (two layers of each). In nine observations, the pupæ were carried 3 times under the red, and 9 times under the yellow glass.

I then put two ants on a paper bridge, the ends supported by pins, the bases of which were in water. The ants wandered backwards and forwards, endeavouring to escape. I then placed the bridge in the dark, and threw the spectrum on it, so that successively the red, yellow, green, blue, and violet rays fell on the bridge.

The ants, however, walked backwards and forwards, without (perhaps from excitement) taking any notice of the colour.

I then allowed some ants (*Lasius niger*) to find some larvæ, to which they obtained access over a narrow paper bridge. When they had got used to it, I arranged so that it passed through a dark box, and threw on it the principal colours of the spectrum—namely, red, yellow, green, blue, and violet, as well as the ultra-red and ultra-violet; but the ants took no notice.

At the suggestion of Prof. Stokes, I then tried the following experiments. Mr. Spottiswoode not only most kindly placed the rich resources of his laboratory at my disposal, but he and his able assistant Mr. Ward were good enough to arrange the apparatus for me.

We tried the ants (*Formica cinerea, Lasius niger*, and *Myrmica ruginodis*) with coloured lights in a Bunsen's burner, using chloride of strontium and carbonate of lithia for red, chloride of barium for green, and chloride of sodium for yellow. The lithium gives an almost pure red, the strontium and barium give a little yellow, but so little that I do not think it would affect the ants.

The yellow of the soda-flame certainly affected the *Formica cinerea*, but the others seemed to take no notice of it.

The barium also affected the *F. cinerea*, but neither of the others; I could not feel sure whether it was the green or the accompanying yellow which disturbed them. The red of the lithium was not so brilliant, still the *F. cinerea* seemed to perceive it.

The strontium-flame did not seem to have any effect on the ants.

It is obvious that these facts suggest a number of interesting inferences. I must, however, repeat the observations, and make others; but we may at least, I think, conclude from the preceding that—(1) ants have the power of distinguishing colour; (2) that they are very sensitive to violet; and it would also seem (3) that their sensations of colour must be very different from those produced upon us.

When I began keeping ants, I surrounded the nests by moats of water. This acted well, but the water required to be continually renewed, especially, of course, in summer, just when the ants were most active. At length, in considering the habits of ants and their relations to flowers, another plan suggested itself to me. The hairs by which plants are clothed fulfil various functions; one is, I believe, to prevent ants and other creeping insects from obtaining access to the flowers, and thus robbing them of their honey.

It occurred to me, therefore, that, instead of water, I might use fur, with the hairs pointing downwards. This I have found to answer perfectly, and I mention it because the same arrangement may perhaps be found practically useful in hot climates. It is very possible, of course, that tropical species of ants might be able to climb up the fur; but at any rate the experiment would be worth trying.

I never succeeded in keeping a bee long under observation. On the other hand, I once kept a wasp (*P. gallica*) for more than nine months. I took her, with her nest, in the Pyrenees, early in May. The nest consisted of about 20 cells, the majority of which contained an egg; but as yet no grubs had been hatched out, and, of course, my wasp was as yet alone in the world. I had no difficulty in inducing her to feed on my hand; but at first she was shy and nervous. She kept her sting in constant readiness, and once or twice in the train, when the officials came for tickets, and I was compelled to hurry her back into the bottle in which she lived, she stung me slightly—I think, however, entirely from fright. Gradually she became quite used to me, and when I took her on my hand apparently expected to be fed. She even allowed me to stroke her without any appearance of fear, and for some months I never saw her sting.

When the cold weather came on, she fell into a drowsy state, and I began to hope she would hibernate and survive the winter. I kept her in a dark place, but watched her carefully, and fed her if ever she seemed at all restless. She came out occasionally, and seemed as well as usual till near the end of February, when one day I observed she had nearly lost the use of her antennæ, though the rest of the body was as usual. She would take no food. Next day I tried again to feed her; but the head seemed dead, though she could still move her legs, wings, and abdomen. The following day I offered her food for the last time; but both head and thorax were dead or paralyzed; she could but wag her tail; a last token, as I could almost fancy, of gratitude and affection. As far as I could judge, her death was quite painless, and she now occupies a place in the British Museum.

As already mentioned, there are certain species of ants in which there are two distinct kinds of workers, doubtless with different functions. But even when all the workers are of one form, it is possible that there is some division of labour. Thus in the autumn of 1875, I noticed an ant belonging to one of my nests of *F. fusca*, out feeding alone. The next day the same ant was again out by herself, and for some weeks no other ant, so far as I observed, came out to the food. I did not, however, watch her with sufficient regularity. One winter, therefore, I kept two nests under close observation, having arranged with my daughters and their governess, Miss Wendland (most conscientious observers), that one of us should look at them once an hour during the day. One of the nests contained about 200 individuals, the other, a nest of *P. rufescens*, with the usual slaves, about 400. The mistresses themselves never come out for food, leaving all this to the slaves.

We began watching on the 1st November, but did not keep an hourly register till the 20th, after which date the results up to the 24th February are given in tables which have been published in the *Linnean Journal*, and in my volume on *Ants, Bees, and Wasps*. The first relates to a nest of *F. fusca*, and the ants are denoted by numbers. An ant marked in my register as No. 3 was at this time acting as feeder to the community. From the time we began to watch, no other ant came to the honey till the 22nd November, when another ant came out, whom we registered as No. 4 : while another on the 28th November was registered as No. 6. These ants were subsequently assisted by five or six others, and in the three months during which the nest was under observation, the supplies for the community were carried in by these few ants.

The second set of observations were made on a nest of *Polyergus* and *F. fusca*. The feeders in this case were, at the beginning of the experiment, those known to us as Nos. 5, 6, and 7. On the 22nd November, a friend, registered as No. 8, came to the honey, and again on the 11th December, but with these two exceptions, the whole of the supplies were carried in by Nos. 5 and 6, with a little help from No. 7.

Thinking now it might be alleged that possibly these were merely unusually active and greedy individuals, I imprisoned No. 6, when she came out to feed on the 5th. As will be seen from the table, no other ant had been out to the honey for some days; and it could therefore hardly be accidental that on that very evening another ant (then registered as No. 9) came out for food. This ant then took the place of No. 6, and (No. 5 being imprisoned on the 11th January) took in all the supplies, again with a little help from No. 7. So matters continued till the 17th, when I imprisoned No. 9, and then again, *i.e.* on the 19th, another ant (No. 10) came out for the food, aided on and after the 22nd by another, No. 11. This seems to me very curious. From the 1st November to the 5th January, with two or three casual exceptions, the whole of the supplies were carried in by three ants, one of whom, however, did comparatively little. The other two were imprisoned, and then, but not till then, a fresh ant appeared on the scene. She carried in the food for a week, and then, she being imprisoned, two others undertook the task. On the other hand, in Nest 1, where the first foragers were not imprisoned, they continued during the whole time to carry the necessary supplies. The facts therefore certainly seem to indicate that certain ants are told off as foragers, and that during winter, when but little food is required, two or three are sufficient to provide it.

I have already mentioned that while *Lasius niger*, the

brown garden-ant, habitually makes use of the out-
of-door Aphides, the yellow meadow-ant keeps the
underground kinds. M. Lespés even considered some
communities of *L. niger* to be more advanced in civilization than others of the same species. He assures us
that if he took specimens of their domestic beetles from
one nest, and placed them in another, always, be it understood, of the same species, the beetles were attacked and
eaten. I have not had the opportunity of repeating
these experiments, but I have moved specimens of the
blind woodlouse, *Platyarthrus*, from one nest to another,
and even from nests of one species to those of another,
and they were always amicably received. But whether
there are differences in advancement within the limits
of the same species or not, there are certainly considerable differences between the different species, and
one may almost fancy that we can trace stages corresponding to the principal steps in the history of human
development.

I do not now refer to slave-making ants, which represent an abnormal, or perhaps only temporary, state of
things, for slavery seems to lead in ants, as in men, to
the degradation of those by whom it is adopted; and
it is not impossible that the slave-making species will
eventually find themselves unable to compete with those
which are more self-dependent, and have reached a
higher phase of civilization. But, putting these slave-
making ants on one side, we find in the different species
of ants different conditions of life, curiously answering
to the earlier stages of human progress. For instance,
some species, such as *Formica fusca*, live principally
on the produce of the chase; for though they feed

partly on the honey-dew of Aphides, they have not domesticated their insects. These ants probably retain the habits once common to all ants. They resemble the lower races of men, who subsist mainly by hunting. Like them, they frequent woods and wilds, live in comparatively small communities, and the instincts of collective action are but little developed among them. They hunt singly, and their battles are single combats, like those of Homeric heroes. Such species as *Lasius flavus* represent a distinctly higher type of social life ; they show more skill in architecture, may literally be said to have domesticated certain species of Aphides, and may be compared to the pastoral stage of human pro- gress—to the races which live on the produce of their flocks and herds. Their communities are more numerous, they act much more in concert, their battles are not mere single combats, but they know how to act in com- bination. I am disposed to hazard the conjecture that they will gradually exterminate the mere hunting species, just as savages disappear before more advanced races. Lastly, agricultural nations may be compared with harvesting ants.

Thus, there seem to be three principal types, offering a curious analogy to the three great phases—the hunting, pastoral, and agricultural stages—in the history of human development.

My experiments certainly seem to indicate the posses- sion by ants of something approaching to language.   It is impossible to doubt that the friends were brought out by the first ant, and as she returned empty-handed to the nest, the others cannot have been induced to follow her by merely observing her proceedings.   In face of such facts as these, it is impossible not to ask ourselves, How far are ants mere exquisite automatons; how far are they conscious beings? When we see an ant-hill, tenanted by thousands of industrious inhabitants, excavating chambers, forming tunnels, making roads, guarding their home, gathering food, feeding the young, tending their domestic animals—each one fulfilling its duties industriously, and without confusion—it is difficult altogether to deny to them the gift of reason; and the preceding observations tend to confirm the opinion that their mental powers differ from those of men not so much in kind as in degree.

Let me in conclusion once more say, that, notwithstanding the labours of those great naturalists to whom I gratefully referred in commencing, it seems to me that there are in natural history few more promising or extensive fields for research than the habits of ants.

LECTURE V.

INTRODUCTION TO THE STUDY OF PREHISTORIC ARCHÆOLOGY.[1]

PREHISTORIC ARCHÆOLOGY has but lately made good its right to recognition as a branch of science; and still, perhaps, there are some who are disposed to question the claim. We can never, they say, become wise beyond what is written: ancient poems and histories contain all that we can ever know about old times and bygone races of men; by the study of antiquities we may often corroborate, and occasionally perhaps even correct, the statements of ancient writers, but beyond this we can never hope to penetrate. The ancient monuments and remains themselves may excite our interest, but can teach us nothing. This opinion is as old as the time of Horace: in one of his best known Odes he tells us that—

> " Vixere fortes ante Agamemnona
> Multi ; sed omnes illacrymabiles
> Urgentur, ignotique longâ
> Nocte, carent quia vate sacro."

---

[1] I have discussed the Antiquity of Man, and his primitive condition in its more material aspects, at greater length in my work on *Prehistoric Times*, and have endeavoured to trace up the course of his social and moral development in a second, *On the Origin of Civilization.*

If this apply to nations as well as to individuals—if our knowledge of the past be confined to that which has been handed down to us in books—then is archæology indeed restrained within fixed and narrow limits; it is reduced to a mere matter of criticism, and almost unworthy to be called a science.

My object in the present address is to vindicate the claims of archæology; to point out briefly the light which has, more particularly in the last few years, been thrown upon the past; and, above all, if possible, to show that the antiquaries of the present day are no visionary enthusiasts, but that the methods of archæological investigation are as trustworthy as those of any natural science. I purposely say the methods, rather than the results; because while I believe that the progress recently made has been mainly due to the use of those methods which have been pursued with so much success in geology, zoology, and other kindred branches of science—and while fully persuaded that in this manner we must eventually ascertain the truth—I readily admit that there are many points on which further evidence is required. Nor need the antiquary be ashamed to own that it is so. Biologists differ about the Darwinian theory; until very lately the emission theory of light was maintained by some of the best authorities; Tyndall and Magnus are at issue as to whether aqueous vapour does or does not absorb heat; astronomers have recently admitted an error of nearly 4,000,000 miles in their estimate of the distance between the earth and the sun; nor is there any single proposition in theology to which a universal assent would be given. Although, therefore, there are no doubt great diversities of opinion among antiquaries, archæology is in this respect only in the same condition as all other branches of knowledge.

Conceding then, frankly, that from several of the following conclusions some good archæologists would entirely dissent, I will now endeavour to state briefly the principal results of modern research, and especially to give, as far as can be done within the limits of a few pages, an idea of the kind of evidence on which these conclusions are based.

I must also add, that my remarks are confined, excepting when it is otherwise specified, to that part of Europe which lies to the north of the Alps ; and that by the Primæval period, I understand that which extended from the first appearance of man down to the commencement of the Christian era.

This period may be divided into four epochs :—Firstly, the Palæolithic, or First Stone Age ; secondly, the Neolithic, or Second Stone Age ; thirdly, the Bronze Age ; and lastly, the Iron Age. Attempts have been made, with more or less success, to establish subdivisions of these periods, but into these I do not now propose to enter : even if we can do no more as yet than establish this succession, that will itself be sufficient to show that we are not entirely dependent upon history.

We will commence, then, with the Palæolithic Age. This is the most ancient period in which we have as yet any decisive proofs of the existence of man. M. Desnoyers some years ago called attention to some bones from the Pliocene beds of St. Prest, which appear to show the marks of knives, and M. l'Abbé Bourgeois has since found in the same locality some flints, which he believes to have been worked by man ; Mr. Whincopp also has in his possession a bone from the crag, which certainly looks as if it had been cut with some sharp instrument. Other archæologists have more recently adduced similar cases. None of them, however, are perfectly conclusive, and as yet the implements found in the river-drift gravels are the oldest undoubted traces of man's existence—older far than any of those in Egypt or Assyria, though belonging to a period which, from a geological point of view, is very recent.

The Palæolithic Age.

As regards the Palæolithic Age, we may, I think, regard the following conclusions as fully borne out by the evidence :—

1. The antiquities referable to this period are usually found in beds of gravel and loam, or, as it is technically called, "loëss," extending along our valleys, and reaching sometimes to a height of 200 feet above the present water-level.

2. These beds were deposited by the existing rivers, which then ran in the same directions as at present, and drained nearly the same areas.

3. With the exception of the coast-line, the geography of Western Europe cannot have been very different at the time those gravels were deposited from what it is now.

4. The fauna of Europe at that time comprised the mammoth, the woolly-haired rhinoceros, the hippopotamus, the urus, the musk-ox, &c., as well as most of the existing animals.

5. The climate was much more extreme, and at times certainly much colder than at present.

6. Though we have no exact measure of time, we can at least satisfy ourselves that this period was one of very great antiquity.

7. Yet man already inhabited Western Europe.

8. He used rude implements of stone ;

9. Which were never polished, and of which some types differ remarkably from any of those that were subsequently in use.

10. He was ignorant of pottery, and (11) of metals.

I will now proceed to examine these eleven conclusions at somewhat greater length :—

1. That these beds of gravel and loam, or, as it is technically called, " loëss," extend along the slopes of the valleys, and reach sometimes to a height of 200 feet above the present water-level, is a mere statement of fact, about which no difference of opinion has arisen.

2. That these beds of gravel and loëss were not deposited by the sea, is proved by the fact that the remains which occur in them are all those of land or fresh-water, and not of marine species. That they were deposited by the existing rivers is evident, because in each river-valley they contain fragments of those rocks only which occur in the area drained by the river itself. As, therefore, the rivers drained the same areas then as now, the geography of Western Europe cannot have been at that period very different from what it is at present.

3. The fauna, however, was very different, the most important species being—*Ursus spelæus* (the cave-bear), *U. priscus, Hyæna spelæa* (the cave-hyæna), *Felis spelæa* (the cave-lion), *Canis lagopus* (the Arctic fox),

Elephas primigenius (the mammoth), *E. antiquus,
Rhinoceros tichorhinus* (the hairy rhinoceros), *R. lepto-
rhinus, R. hemitæchus, Hippopotamus major* (the hippopotamus), *Ovibos moschatus* (the musk ox), *Megaceros
hibernicus* (the Irish elk), *E. fossilis* (the wild horse),
Gulo luscus (the glutton), *Cervus tarandus* (the reindeer),
Bison Europæus (the aurochs), *Bos primigenius* (the
urus); besides some smaller, but still very interesting
species.

4. The greater severity of the climate is indicated
by the nature of the fauna.   The musk-ox, the woolly-
haired rhinoceros, the mammoth, the lemming, &c., are
Arctic species, and the reindeer then extended to the
South of France.   Another argument is derived from
the presence of great sandstone blocks in the gravels of
some rivers, as, for instance, of the Somme : these, it
appears, must have been transported by ice.[1]   On the
other hand, the geological evidence, together with the
presence of the hippopotamus, and other southern species,
indicates that the cold was not continuous, but that warm
periods intervened.

5. The great antiquity of the period now under
discussion is evident from several considerations.   The
extinction of the large mammalia must have been a
work of time ; and neither in the earliest writings, nor
in the vaguest traditions, do we find any indication of
their presence in Western Europe.   Still more conclusive
evidence is afforded by the condition of our valleys.
The beds of gravel and loam cannot have been deposited

---

[1] Since this lecture was written two excellent works have been
published on this part of the subject—Geikie's *Great Ice Age,* and
Croll's *Climate and Time.*

by any sudden cataclysm, both on account of their
regularity, and also of the fact, already mentioned, that
the materials of one river-system are never mixed with
those of another. To take an instance. The gravel of
the Somme valley is entirely formed of débris from the
chalk and tertiary strata occupying that area; but at
a right angle to, and within a very few miles of, the
headwaters of the Somme, comes the valley of the Oise.
In this valley are other older strata, no fragments of
which have found their way into the Somme valley,
though they could not have failed to do so, had the
gravels in question been the result of any great cataclysm, or had the Somme then drained a larger area
than at present. The beds in question are found in
some cases 200 feet above the present water-level, and
the bottom of the valley is occupied by a bed of peat,
which in some places is as much as 30 feet in thickness.
We have no means of making an accurate calculation;
but even if we allow, as we must, a good deal for the
floods which would be produced by the melting of the
snow, still it is evident that for the excavation of the
valley by the river to a depth of more than 200 feet,[1]
and then for the formation of so thick a bed of peat,
much time must have been required. If, moreover, we
consider the alteration which has taken place in the
climate, as well as in the fauna; and, finally, remember
also that the last eighteen hundred years have produced
scarcely any perceptible change, we cannot but come to
the conclusion that many, very many, centuries have

---

[1] Many persons find a difficulty in understanding how the river
could have deposited gravel at so great a height, forgetting that the
valley was not then excavated to anything like its present depth.

elapsed since the river ran at a level so much higher than the present, and the country was occupied by a fauna so unlike that now in existence there.

6. The presence of man is proved by the discovery of stone implements [1] (Figs. 55 and 56). Strictly speaking, these only prove the presence of reasoning beings ; but this being granted, few, if any, would doubt that the beings in question were men. Human bones, moreover, have been found in cave-deposits, which, in the opinion of the best judges, belonged to this period ; and M. Boucher de Perthes considers that various fragments of human bone found at Moulin Quignon are also genuine. On this point long discussions have taken place, into which I will not now enter. The question before us is, whether men existed at all, not whether they had bones. On the latter point no dispute is likely to arise, and as regards the former, the works of man are as good evidence as his bones could be. Moreover, there seems to me nothing wonderful in the great scarcity of human bones. A country where the inhabitants subsist on the produce of the chase can never be otherwise than scantily peopled. If we admit that for each man there must be a thousand head of game existing at any one time—and this seems a moderate allowance ; remembering also that most mammalia are less long-lived than men, we should naturally expect to find human remains very rare as compared with those of other animals. Among a people who burnt their dead, of course this disproportion would be immensely increased. That the flint implements found in these gravels *are* implements it is unnecessary

[1] For a general account of stone implements I may refer to Mr. Evans's admirable work on that subject.

to argue. Their regularity, and the care with which
they have been worked to an edge, prove that they have

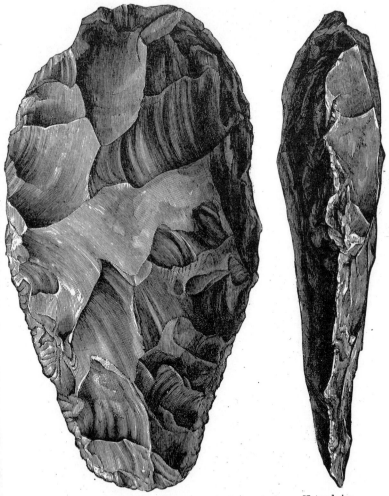

Fig. 55.—Flint Implement from St. Acheul, near Amiens.   Natural size.
(*In my collection.*)

been *intentionally* chipped into their present forms, and
arc not the result of accident.   That they are not

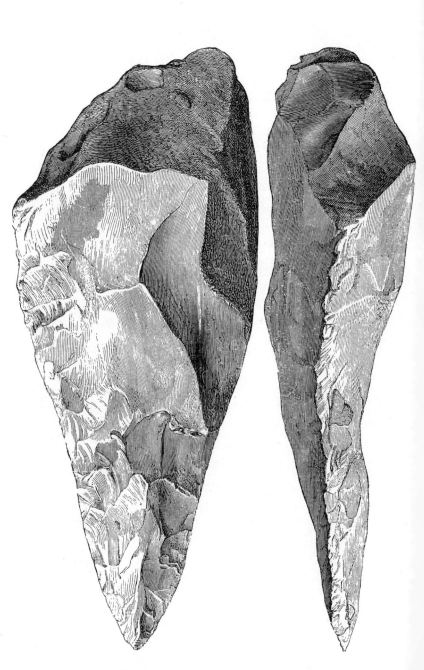

FIG. 56.—Flint Implement from St. Acheul, near Amiens.   Natural size.
(*In my collection.*)

forgeries we may be certain : firstly, because they have
been found *in situ* by many excellent observers—by all,
in fact, who have looked perseveringly for them ; and
secondly, because, as the discolouration of their surface is
quite superficial, and follows the existing outline, it has
evidently been produced since the flints were brought to
their present forms.   This is
clearly shown in Fig. 57, which
represents a fractured surface
of Fig. 56, and shows the dark
natural flint surrounded by
the altered surface.   The forgeries—for there *are* forgeries
—are of a dull lead colour,
like other freshly-broken surfaces of flint.   The same evidence justifies us in concluding
that the implements are coeval
with the beds of gravel in which
they are found.

7. Without counting flakes,
several thousand flint implements of the Palæolithic Age
have been discovered in northern France and southern Eng-

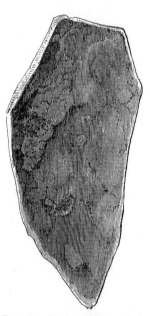

FIG. 57.—Section of Fig. 56 showing discolouration of surface.

land.   These are all of types which differ considerably
from those which came subsequently into use, and they
are none of them polished ; we may therefore, I think,
infer that the art of polishing stone implements was as
yet unknown.

8 and 9.   In the same manner, I think, we may
safely conclude that the use of metal and of pottery

was then unknown, as is the case even now with many races of savages.

Although flint implements were observed in the drift-gravels more than half a century ago by Mr. Frere, still his observations were forgotten until the same discovery was again made by M. Boucher de Perthes. For our knowledge of the gravel-beds in which they occur, however, we are principally indebted to Mr. Prestwich. Sir Charles Lyell has the high merit of having carefully examined the facts, and given to the antiquity of man the authority of his great name; nor must the labours of Mr. Evans be passed unnoticed. To him we owe the first comparison between the flint implements of this and those of the Neolithic period.

As long ago as 1828 MM. Tournal and Christol found in the caves of the south of France human remains associated with those of extinct animals, and shortly afterwards M. Schmerling made similar observations in Belgium. Kent's Hole, near Torquay, was carefully examined by Mr. McEvery in 1825, but his researches remained in manuscript until they were published by Mr. Vivian in 1859. In 1840, however, Mr. Godwin Austin had also made researches in Kent's Hole, and convinced himself that man co-existed in this country with the mammoth, &c. Since that time various caverns have been examined most carefully by Christy, Lartet, Falconer, Dupont, Busk, Powelly, Boyd Dawkins, Sandford, Mirk, Tiddeman, &c. To Mr. Boyd Dawkins, moreover, we are indebted for a special work on *Cave Hunting*.

The general facts may be stated to be, that while thousands of implements made out of stone, bone, and horn, have been collected, no trace of pottery, nor evidence of the use of metals, not even a polished stone implement, has yet been met with. The people who lived in the South of France at that period seem, in a great many respects, to have resembled the Esquimaux. Their principal food was the reindeer, and though traces of the musk-ox, mammoth, cave-lion, as well as other animals of the quaternary fauna have been met with, it is still possible that these may not belong to the same period. These cavemen were very ingenious, and excellent workers in flint; but though their bone-pins, &c., are beautifully polished, this is never the case with their flint weapons. The habit of allowing offal and bones to accumulate in their dwellings is indicative, probably, of a cold climate.

Perhaps, however, the most remarkable fact of all is, that although in other respects so slightly advanced in civilization, these ancient French cavemen, like the Esquimaux, show a wonderful genius for art. Many very spirited drawings of animals have been found represented on fragments of bone, stone, and horn, and M. Lartet has found in the rock-shelter at La Madelaine a fragment of mammoth-tusk, on which was engraved a representation of the animal itself.

The Neolithic Age.

We now pass to the later Stone or Neolithic Age, with reference to which the following propositions may, I think, be regarded as satisfactorily established :—

1. There was a period when polished stone axes were extensively used in Europe.

2. The objects belonging to this period do not occur in the river-drift gravel-beds ;

3. Nor in association with the great extinct mammalia.

4. They were in use long before the discovery or introduction of metals.

5. The Danish shell-mounds, or Kjökkenmöddings, belong to this period ;

6. As do many of the Swiss lake-dwellings ;

7. And of the tumuli, or burial-mounds.

8. Rude stone implements appear to have been in use longer than those more carefully worked.

9. Hand-made pottery was in use during this period.

10. In Central Europe the ox, sheep, goat, pig, and dog were already domesticated.

11. Agriculture had also commenced.

12. Flax was cultivated and woven into tissues.

13. At least two distinct races already occupied Western Europe.

1. That there was a period when polished axes and other implements of stone were extensively used in Western Europe is sufficiently proved by the great numbers in which these objects occur : for instance, the Dublin Museum contains more than 2,000, that of Copenhagen more than 10,000, and that of Stockholm not fewer than 15,000.

2. The objects characteristic of this period do not occur in the river-drift gravels. Some of the simpler ones, indeed—as, for instance, flint-flakes—were used both in the Neolithic and Palæolithic periods, and indeed much later. The polished axes, chisels, gouges, &c., are very distinct, however, from the ruder implements of

the Palæolithic Age, and are never found in the river-drift gravels. Conversely, the Palæolithic types have never yet been met with in association with those characteristic of the later epoch.

Again, while the Neolithic implements are remarkably numerous in Denmark and Sweden, the Palæolithic types are absolutely unknown there, as well as in Eastern Europe. It is probable, therefore, that the northern part of our Continent was not inhabited by man during the earlier period.

3. Nor do the types of the Neolithic age ever occur in company with the mammoth, *Rhinoceros tichorinus*, and other animals characteristic of the Quaternary fauna, under circumstances which would justify us in regarding them as coeval.

4. The implements in question were in use before the introduction or discovery of metal. It is a great mistake to suppose that implements of stone were abandoned directly metal was discovered. For certain purposes, as for arrow-heads, stone would be quite as suitable as the more precious substance. Flint flakes, moreover, were so useful, and so easily obtained, that they were occasionally employed even down to a very late period. Even for axes and chisels, the incontestable superiority of metal was counterbalanced for a while by its greater costliness. Captain Cook, indeed, tells us that in Tahiti the implements of stone and bone were in a very few years replaced by those of metal; a stone hatchet was then, he says, "as rare a thing as an iron one was eight years ago, and a chisel of bone or stone is not to be seen." The rapidity with which the change from stone to metal is effected depends upon the supply

of the latter. In the above case Cook had with him an abundance of metal, in exchange for which the islanders supplied his vessels with great quantities of fresh meat, vegetables, and other more questionable articles of merchandize. The introduction of metal into Europe was certainly far more gradual; stone and metal were long used side by side, and it would be unsafe to refer every stone implement to the Stone Age. It would be easy to quote numerous instances in which implements have been, without any sufficient reason, referred to the Stone Age, merely because they were formed of stone. The two Stone Ages are characterized not merely by the use of stone, but by the use of stone to the exclusion of metal. I cannot therefore too strongly impress on archæologists *that many stone implements belong to the metallic period.* Why, then, it will be asked, may they not all have done so? and this question I will now endeavour to answer.

5. The Danish shell-mounds are the refuse heaps of the ancient inhabitants round whose dwellings the bones and shells of the animals on which they fed gradually accumulated. Like a modern dustheap, these shell-mounds contain all kinds of household objects—some purposely thrown away as useless, but some also accidentally lost. These mounds have been examined with great care by the Danish archæologists, and especially by Professor Steenstrup. Many thousand implements of stone and bone have been obtained from them; and as, on the one hand, from the absence of extinct animals,[1] and of implements belonging to the Palæo-

---

[1] The Reindeer also, which at an earlier period was common in central Europe, is entirely absent.

lithic Age, we conclude that these shell-mounds do not belong to that period, so, on the other hand, from the absence of all trace of metal, we are justified in referring them to a period when metal was unknown.

6. The same arguments apply to some of the Swiss lake-dwellings, the discovery of which we owe to Dr. Keller,[1] and which have been so admirably studied by Desor, Morlot, Troyon, and other Swiss archæologists. A glance at the Table A will show that, while in some of them objects of metal are very abundant, in others, which have been not less carefully or thoughtfully explored, stone implements are met with to the exclusion of metallic ones. It may occur, perhaps, to some, that the absence of metal in some of the lake-villages, and its presence in others, is to be accounted for by its scarcity—that, in fact, metal will be found when the localities shall have been sufficiently searched. But a glance at the table will show that the settlements in which metal occurs are deficient in stone implements. Take the same number of objects from Wangen and Nidau, and in the one case 90 per cent. will be of metal, while in the other the whole number are of stone or bone. This cannot be accidental—the numbers are too great to admit of such a hypothesis; nor can the fact be accounted for by contemporaneous differences of civilization, because the localities are too close together; neither is it an affair of wealth, because we find such articles as fishhooks, &c., made of metal.

7. We may also, I think, safely refer some of the tumuli or burial mounds to this period. When we find

---

[1] Dr. Keller's *Memoirs* have been collected and translated into English by Mr. Lee.

a large tumulus, the erection of which must have been extremely laborious, it is evident that it must have been erected in honour of some distinguished individual ; and when his flint daggers, axes, &c.—which, from the labour and difficulty of making them, must have been of great value—were deposited in the tomb, it is reasonable to conclude that if he had possessed any arms of metal, they also would have been buried with him. This we know was done in subsequent periods. In burials of the Stone Age the corpse was either deposited in a sitting posture, or burnt, but rarely, if ever, extended at full length.[1]

8. It is an error to suppose that the rudest flint implements are necessarily the oldest. The Palæolithic implements show admirable workmanship. Moreover, every flint instrument is rude at first. A bronze celt may be cast perfect ; but a flint implement is rudely blocked out in the first instance, and then, if any concealed flaw comes to light, or if any ill-directed blow causes an inconvenient fracture, the unfinished implement is perhaps thrown away. Moreover, the simplest flint-flake forms a capital knife, and accordingly we find that some simple stone implements were in use long after metal had replaced the beautifully-worked axes, knives, and daggers, which must always have been very difficult to make. The period immediately before the introduction of metal may reasonably be supposed to be that of the best stone implements, but the use of the

---

[1] For accounts of tumuli belonging to this period see Hoare's *Ancient Wiltshire*, Nilsson's *Stone Age*, Warne's *Ancient Dorset*, Bateman's *Antiquities of Derbyshire*, and *Ten Years' Diggings*, Borlase's *Nenia Cornubiæ*, Greenwell's *British Barrows*, &c.

simpler ones lingered long. Moreover, there are some reasons to believe that pierced stone axes are characteristic of the early metallic period.

9. Hand-made pottery is abundant in the shell-mounds and the lake-villages, as well as in the tumuli which appear to belong to the Stone Age. No conclusive evidence that the potter's wheel was yet in use has been discovered.

10. The animals characteristic of the Palæolithic period have disappeared. Even the reindeer has retreated from Central Europe.

11. The dog is the only domestic animal found in the shell-mounds; but remains of the ox, sheep, goat, and pig appear in the lake-villages. There is some doubt about the horse; and the barn-door fowl, as well as the cat, was unknown.

12. The presence of corn-crushers, as well as of carbonized wheat, barley, and flax, in the Swiss lake-dwellings, proves that agriculture was already pursued with success in Central Europe. Oats, rye, and hemp were unknown.

13. Tissues of woven flax have been found in some of the Swiss lake-villages.

14. At least two forms of skull, one long and one round, are found in the tumuli which appear to belong to this period. Until now, however, we have not a single human skull from the Danish shell-mounds, nor from any Swiss lake-dwelling, which can be referred with certainty to this period.

The Bronze Age.

1. The Neolithic Age was followed by a period when bronze was extensively used for arms and implements.

2. Stone, however, was also in use, especially for certain purposes ; as, for instance, for arrow-heads, and in the form of flakes for cutting.

3. Some of the bronze axes appear to be mere copies of the earlier stone ones.

4. Many of the Swiss lake-villages and of the tumuli belong to this period.

5. This is shown, not merely by the presence of metal, but also by other considerations.

6. The pottery of the Bronze Age is better than that of the earlier period.

7. Gold, amber, and glass, were used for ornamental purposes.

8. Silver, lead, and zinc appear to have been unknown.

9. This was also the case with iron.

10. Coins were not in use.

11. Skins were probably worn, but tissues of flax and wool were also in use.

12. The ornamentation of the period is characteristic, and consists of geometrical markings.

13. The handles of the arms, the bracelets, &c., indicate a small race.

14. Writing appears to have been unknown ;

15. Yet there was a very considerable commerce.

16. It is more than probable that the knowledge of bronze was introduced into, not discovered in, Europe.

1. It is admitted by all that there was a period when bronze was extensively used for arms and implements. The great number of such objects which are preserved in our museums places this beyond doubt. For France alone Monsieur Chantre, in his *Age du Bronze*, gives the following numbers:—Celts, 9,153; swords and daggers, 727; lances, 513; knives, 342; sickles, 225; pins, 1,220; needles, 204; bracelets, 1,086; rings and chains, 1,572; arrow-heads, 213; hammers, 23; anvils, 5; chisels, 58; gouges, 31; razors, 62; saws, 8; hooks, 172; moulds, 74; and a variety of other articles, making altogether no less than 20,000 objects. In Switzerland, again, more than 10,000 have been discovered: the numbers for some of the principal lake-villages are given in Table B.[1]

2. It would, however, be a mistake to suppose that stone implements were entirely abandoned. Arrow-heads and flakes of flint are found abundantly in some of those Swiss lake-villages which contain bronze. In these cases, indeed, it may be argued, that the same site had been occupied both before and after the introduction of bronze. The evidence derived from the examination of tumuli is, however, not open to the same objection, and in these objects of bronze and of stone are very frequently found together. Thus I have shown, by an analysis of the investigations recorded by Mr. Bateman, that in three-fourths of the tumuli containing bronze (29 out of 37) stone objects also occurred.

3. Some of the bronze axes appear to be mere copies of the stone ones. Such simple axes of iron are still used in Central Africa, where no evidence of a Bronze

---

[1] All these numbers might now be largely increased.

Age has yet been found, but in Europe they are not met with.

4. Many of the Swiss lake-villages belong to this period. The Table B (very kindly drawn up, at my request, by Dr. Keller) places this beyond a doubt, and gives a good idea of the objects in use during the Bronze Age, and the state of civilization during that period.

5. The absence of metal, though the principal, is by no means the only point which distinguishes the Stone Age villages from those of the Bronze period. If we compare Nidau, as a type of the last, with Moosseedorf, as the best representative of the former, we shall find that, while bones of wild animals preponderate in the one, those of tame ones are most numerous in the latter. The vegetable remains point also to the same conclusion. Even if we knew nothing about the want of metal in the older lake-villages, we should still, says Professor Heer, be compelled from botanical considerations to admit their greater antiquity.

Moreover, so far as they have been examined, the piles themselves tell the same tale. Those of the Bronze Age settlements were evidently cut with metal; those of the earlier villages with stone, or at any rate with rude and blunt instruments.

6. The pottery was much better than that of the earlier period. A great deal of it was still hand-made, but some is said to show marks of the potter's wheel.

7. Gold, amber, and glass, were used for ornamental purposes.

8. Silver, zinc, and lead, on the contrary, were apparently unknown.

9. The same appears to have been the case with iron.

10. Coins have never been found with bronze arms. To this rule I only know of three apparent exceptions. Not a single coin has been met with in any of the Swiss lake-villages of this period.

11. The dress of this period no doubt still consisted in great part of skins. Tissues of flax have been found, however, in some of the lake-villages, and fragments of woollen material have been found in tumuli, nay, in one case, a whole suit (consisting of a cloak, a shirt, two shawls, a pair of leggings, and two caps) was found in a Danish tumulus which evidently belonged to the Bronze Age; as it contained a sword, a brooch, a knife, an awl, a pair of tweezers, and a large stud, all of bronze, besides a small button of tin, a javelin-head of flint, a bone comb, and a bark box.

We have independent evidence of the same fact in the presence of spindle-whorls.

12. The ornamentation on the arms, implements, and pottery is peculiar. It consists of geometrical patterns —straight lines, circles, triangles, zigzags, &c. Animals and vegetables are very rarely attempted, and never with success.

13. Another peculiarity of the bronze arms lies in the small size of the handles. The same observation applies to the bracelets, &c. They could not be used by the present inhabitants of Northern Europe.

14. No traces of writing have been met with in any finds of the Bronze Age. There is not an inscription on any of the arms or pottery found in the Swiss lake-villages, and I only know one instance of a bronze cutting instrument with letters on it.

15. The very existence of bronze appears to indicate

that of a considerable and extensive commerce, inasmuch as there are only two places—namely, Cornwall and the Island of Banca—whence tin can have been obtained in large quantities. There are, indeed, some other places where it occurs, as, for instance, Spain, Saxony, and Brittany, but only (now at least) in small amounts, though possibly it may once have been more abundant. The earliest source of tin, was not, I think, any one of those now known to us, but it is probable that for many centuries before our era, the principal supply was derived from Cornwall. The intercourse then existing between different parts of Europe is also proved by the great, not to say complete, similarity of the arms from very different parts of Europe.

16. Finally, as copper must have been in use before bronze, and as arms and implements of that metal are almost unknown in Western Europe, it is reasonable to conclude that the knowledge of bronze was introduced into, not discovered in, Europe.

Archæologists are, however, by no means agreed as to the race by whom these bronze weapons were made, or at least used. Mr. Wright, for instance, attributed them to the Romans, Professor Nilsson to the Phœnicians. The first of these theories I believe to be utterly untenable. In addition to the facts already brought forward, there are two which by themselves are almost sufficient to disprove the hypothesis. Firstly, the word *ferrum* was employed in Latin as a synonym for a sword. This would scarcely have been the case if another metal had been generally used for the purpose. Secondly, the distribution of bronze weapons and implements does not favour such a theory. The Romans never entered

Denmark ; it has been doubted whether they ever landed in Ireland. Yet, while more than 350 bronze swords have been found in Denmark, and a very large number in Ireland also,[1] I have only been able to hear of about fifty bronze swords found in Italy. The rich museums at Florence, Rome, and Naples, do not appear to contain any of those typical, leaf-shaped bronze swords, which are, comparatively speaking, so common in the North. That bronze swords should have been introduced into Denmark by a people who never occupied that country, and from a part of Europe in which they are so rare, is surely a most untenable hypothesis. It is doubtless true that a few cases are on record in which bronze weapons are said to have been, and very likely were, found in association with Roman remains. Mr. Wright has pointed out three, none of which seem to me clearly established, while one of them is clearly not a case in point. But, under any circumstances, we must expect to meet with some such instances. My only wonder is that so few of them exist.

As regards Professor Nilsson's theory, according to which the Bronze Age objects are of Phœnician origin, I will only say that the Phœnicians in historical times were well acquainted with iron, and that their favourite ornamentation was of a different character from that of the Bronze Age. If, then, Professor Nilsson be correct, the bronze weapons must belong to an earlier period in Phœnician history than that with which we are partially familiar.

[1] The Museum at Dublin contains 282 swords and daggers : unluckily, the number of swords is not stated separately.

It would now be natural that I should pass on to the Iron Age, but the transition period between the two is illustrated by a discovery so remarkable that I cannot pass it over altogether in silence. M. Ramsauer, for many years head of the salt-mines at Hallstadt, near Salzburg, in Austria, has opened not less than 980 graves in a country apparently belonging to an ancient colony of miners. The results comprise about 4,000 objects of bronze, and 600 of iron. The following table (p. 173) gives M. Ramsauer's figures, but the numbers have since been considerably increased.

That the period to which these graves belonged was that of the transition between the Bronze and Iron Ages, is evident, both because we find cutting instruments of iron as well as of bronze, and also because both are of somewhat unusual, and we may almost say of intermediate, types. The same remark applies to the ornamentation. Animals are frequently represented, but very poorly executed, while geometrical patterns are well drawn. Coins are entirely absent. That the transition was from bronze to iron, and not from iron to bronze, is clear; because here, as elsewhere, while iron instruments with bronze handles are common, there is not a single case of a bronze blade with an iron handle. This shows that when both metals were in use, iron was preferred for blades. Another interesting point in the Hallstadt Bronze is the absence of silver, lead, and zinc (excepting, of course, as a mere impurity in the bronze). This is the more remarkable, inasmuch as the presence, not only of tin itself, but also of glass, amber, and ivory, indicates the existence of an extensive commerce.

The Iron Age.

The Iron Age is the period when this metal was first used for weapons and cutting instruments. During this epoch we emerge into the broad, but in many respects delusive, glare of history.

No one of course will deny that arms of iron were in use by our ancestors at the time of the Roman invasion.

I have already attempted to show, from the frequent occurrence of iron blades with bronze handles, and the entire absence of the reverse, that iron must have succeeded and replaced bronze. Other arguments might be adduced ; but it will be sufficient to state broadly that which I think no experienced archæologist will deny—namely, that the objects which accompany bronze weapons are much more archaic in character than those which are found with weapons of iron.

That the bronze swords and daggers were not used by the Romans in Cæsar's times, I have already attempted to prove. That they were not used at that period by the northern races is distinctly stated in history. I will, however, endeavour also to make this evident on purely archæological grounds. We have several important finds of this period, among which I may specially call attention to the lake-village of La Tene, in the Lake of Neufchâtel. At this place no flint implements (excepting flakes) have occurred. Only fifteen objects of bronze have been found, and only one of them was an axe. Moreover this was pierced for a handle, and belonged therefore to a form rarely, if ever, occurring in finds of the Bronze Age. On the other hand, the objects of iron are numerous, and comprise fifty swords, twenty-three lances, and five axes. Coins have also been met with at this station, while they are entirely absent in those of the Bronze Age.

The only other find of the Iron Age to which I will now refer is that of Nydam, recently described at length by M. Engelhardt in his excellent work on *Denmark in the Early Iron Age*. At this place have been found an immense number of the most diverse objects—clothes, brooches, tweezers, beads, helmets, shields, coats of mail, buckles, harness, boats, rakes, brooms, mallets, bows, vessels of wood and pottery, 80 knives, 30 axes, 40 awls, 160 arrow-heads, 180 swords, and nearly 600 lances. All these weapons were of iron, though bronze was freely used for ornaments. That this find, as well as the very similar one at Thorsbjerg, in the same neighbourhood, belonged to the Roman period, is clearly proved by the existence of numerous coins belonging to the first two centuries after Christ, although not one has occurred in any of the Bronze Age lake-villages, or in the great find at Hallstadt.

It is quite clear, therefore, that neither bronze nor stone weapons were in use in Northern Europe at the commencement of our era.

A closer examination would much strengthen this conclusion. For instance, at Thorsbjerg alone there are seven inscriptions, either in Runes or Roman characters ; while, as I have already stated, letters are quite unknown, with one exception, on any object of the Bronze Age, or in the great transition find at Hallstadt. Again, the significance of the absence of silver in the Hallstadt find is greatly increased when we see that in the true

Iron Age, as in the Nydam and other similar finds, silver was used to ornament shield-bosses, shield-rims, sandals, brooches, breast-plates, sword-hilts, sword-sheaths, girdles, harness, &c. ; and also for clasps, pendants, boxes, and tweezers ; while in one case a helmet was made of this comparatively rare material.

The pottery also shows much improvement, the forms of the weapons are quite different, and the character of the ornamentation is very unlike, and much more advanced than that of the Bronze Age. Moreover, the bronze used in the Iron Age differs from that of the Bronze Age, in that it frequently contains lead and zinc in considerable quantities. These metals have never been found, excepting as mere impurities, in the bronzes of the true Bronze Age, nor even in those of Hallstadt.

These finds, moreover, clearly show that the inhabitants of Northern and Western Europe were by no means such mere savages as we have been apt to suppose. As far as our own ancestors are concerned, this is rendered even more evident by the discoveries of those ancient British coins which have been so well described and figured by Mr. John Evans.[1]

In conclusion, I would venture to suggest that some steps ought to be taken to provide for the preservation of our ancient National Antiquities. We cannot put Stonehenge or the Wansdyke into a museum—all the more reason why we should watch over them where they are ; and even if the destruction of our ancient monuments should, under any circumstances, become necessary, careful drawings ought first to be made, and their

[1] *The Coins of the Ancient Britons.*

removal should take place under proper superintendence. We are apt to blame the Eastern peasants who use the grand old monuments of Egypt or Assyria as mere stone-quarries, but we forget that even in our own country, Avebury, the most magnificent of Druidical remains, was almost destroyed for the profit of a few pounds; while recently the Jockey Club has mutilated the remaining portion of the Devil's Dyke on Newmarket Heath, in order to make a bank for the exclusion of scouts at trial races. In this case, also, the saving, if any, must have been very small; and I am sure that no society of English gentlemen would have sanctioned such a proceeding, had they given the subject a moment's consideration.

In this short Introduction I have purposely avoided all reference to history, and the use of historical data, because I have been particularly anxious to show that in Archæology we can arrive at definite and satisfactory conclusions on independent grounds, without any such assistance; consequently, regarding times before writing was invented, and therefore before written history had commenced.

I have endeavoured to select only those arguments which rest on well-authenticated facts. For my own part, however, I care less about the results than about the method. For an infant science, as for a child, it is of small importance to make rapid strides at first: and while I believe that our present views will stand the test of further investigations, it is of the greatest importance that our method should be one which will eventually lead us to the truth.

TABLE A.

	STONE					BRONZE								IRON							COINS
	Axes	Arrows	Flakes, &c.	Other Objects	Total	Axes	Knives	Lances	Sickles	Fish-hooks	Ornaments	Sundries	Total	Swords	Axes	Knives	Lances	Ornaments	Sundries	Total	
SWITZERLAND																					
Wangen	1500	—	2500	450	4450	—	:	:	—	—	—	—	—	—	—	—	—	—	—	—	0
Moosseedorf	100	25	2300	277	2702	—	:	:	—	—	—	—	—	—	—	—	—	—	—	—	0
Nussdorf	1000	100	100	30	1230	—	:	—	—	—	—	—	—	—	—	—	—	—	—	—	0
Wauwyl	43	36	200	147	426	—	:	—	—	—	—	—	—	—	—	—	—	—	—	—	0
Nidau	33	—	—	335 Corn Crushers	368	23	102	27	18	109	1420	305	2004	—	—	—	—	—	—	—	0
Cortaillod	—	—	—	Corn Crushers	—	13	22	4	2	71	515	208	835	—	—	—	—	—	—	—	0
Estavayer	—	—	—	Many corn crushers	—	6	14	—	1	43	403	150	617	—	—	—	—	—	—	—	0
Corcelettes	—	—	—		—	1	19	2	7	—	465	16	510	—	—	—	—	—	—	—	0
Morges	—	—	—		—	50	20	11	11	10	108	?	210	—	—	—	—	—	1	1	0
Marin	—	33	Some	12 Balls	—	1 Pierced	—	—	—	—	1	13	15	50	5	4	23	More than 100	61	250	9
Larnaud	—	—	—	—	—	87	76	54	51	6	768	758	1800	—	—	—	—	—	—	—	0
Reallon	—	—	—	—	—	—	1	2	2	—	447	1	453	—	—	—	—	—	—	—	0
DENMARK																					
Nydam	—	—	—	A few Whetstones	—	—	—	—	—	—	—	Ornaments very numerous	—	100	30	86	500 at least	?	300 at least	1000 at least	34

TABLE B.

	Nidau.	Mœrigen.	Estavayer.	Cortaillod.	Corcelettes.	Auvernier.	Other places.	TOTAL.
Celts and fragments . .	23	7	6	13	1	6	11	67
Swords	—	—	—	—	—	—	4	4
Hammers	4	—	1	—	—	—	—	5
Knives and fragments .	102	19	14	22	19	8	9	193
Pins	611	53	239	183	237	22	22	1,367
Small rings	496	28	115	195	202	14	3	1,053
Earrings	238	42	36	116	—	3	5	440
Bracelets and fragments .	55	14	16	21	26	11	2	145
Fish-hooks	189	12	43	71	9	2	1	248
Awls	95	3	49	98	17	—	—	262
Spiral wires	—	—	46	50	5	—	—	101
Lance-heads	27	7	—	4	2	5	2	47
Arrow-heads	—	—	5	1	—	—	—	6
Buttons.	—	1	28	10	10	—	—	49
Needles	20	2	3	4	1	—	—	30
Various ornaments . .	15	5	7	18	3	1	—	49
Saws . . . . . , . .	—	—	3	—	—	—	—	3
Daggers	—	—	—	—	—	—	2	2
Sickles	18	12	1	2	7	1	4	45
Double-pointed pins . .	75	—	—	—	—	—	—.	75
Small bracelets	20	—	—	11	—	—	—	31
Sundries	96	3	5	16	—	—	4	124
TOTAL	2084	208	617	835	539	73	69	4,346

TABLE C.

GRAVES WITH BODIES BURIED IN THE ORDINARY MANNER.

ANTIQUITIES.

	No. of the Graves.	Gold Ornaments.	Bronze.				Iron.		Ornaments.		Pottery.	Stone.
			Ornamnts	Vessels.	Sundries.	Weapons.	Weapons.	Other Objects.	Amber.	Glass.		
HALLSTADT	527	6	1471	3	35	18	161	33	165	38	334	57

GRAVES WITH BURNT CORPSES.

ANTIQUITIES.

	No. of the Graves.	Gold Ornaments.	Bronze.				Iron.		Ornaments.		Pottery.	Different Objects.	
			Ornamnts	Vessels.	Sundries.	Weapons.	Weapons.	Other Objects.	Amber.	Glass.			
	453	58	1744	179	54	91	349	41	105	35	908	100	
TOTALS	980	64	3215	182	89	109	510	74	270	73	1242	157	5985

LECTURE VI.

WHEN your excellent Secretary, Mr. Smith, first communicated to me the wish of your Committee that I should become your President for this year, I must confess to some natural hesitation in accepting your very flattering invitation. I have so recently become directly connected with the county, there are so many gentlemen well qualified, not only to fill, but to adorn the office, that I could not but be doubtful how far the suggestion would be approved by, and advantageous to, the Society. Nevertheless I have long felt so deep an interest in this, the central, and, archæologically, the richest district of England, I am always so happy in the sunshine of your glorious downs, or under the shadow of your beautiful cathedral, that I could not refuse myself the pleasure, and—for it is never very difficult to convince one's self of what one wishes to believe—it seemed to me that the responsibility of the selection would after all in no sense rest upon me.

It is indeed always a pleasure to come into Wiltshire, and much more too than a mere idle one. I sometimes think that every one—at any rate, every Schoolmaster and every Member of Parliament, ought to make the tour of the county and visit its principal antiquities.

There are still many who go abroad to visit distant antiquities, neglecting those at home, like the "Wander Witt of Wiltshire," mentioned by Gibbons in 1670, who, having "screwed" himself into the company of some Roman antiquaries, confessed that he had never seen Stonage, as he calls it, "whereupon they kicked him out of doors, and bade him goe home and see Stonage; and I wish," adds Gibbons, "all such Æsopicall cocks, as slight these admired stones, and other our domestick monuments (by which they might be admonished to eschew some evil, and doe some good,) and scrape for barley cornes of vanity out of forreigne dunghills, might be handled, or rather footed, as he was."

Indeed, it would be difficult to find a pleasanter or more instructive tour. The visitor would begin, perhaps, with Marlborough, pass the large Castle Mound, and coming soon within sight of the grand hill of Silbury, leave the high road and drive, partly up the ancient roadway, into the venerable circle of Abury, perhaps the most interesting of our great national monuments.

There he would walk round the ancient vallum, he would search out the remaining stones among the cottages and farmsteads, and wonder at the mechanical skill which could have moved such ponderous masses; and at the modern barbarism which could have destroyed such interesting, I might almost say sacred, monuments of the past.

From Abury he would pass on across the great wall of Wansdyke, which he would trace on each side of the road, stretching away as far as the eye could reach, and he would sleep at the ancient city of the Devizes.

On Salisbury Plain he would visit Stonehenge, the

sanctity of which is attested, not only by its own evidence, but by the tumuli which cluster reverently round it. At old Sarum he would for the first time come across real and written history. Lastly, at Salisbury he would see one of our most beautiful Cathedrals, and an excellent Museum, which we owe to the liberality of Dr. Blackmore, while for the admirable arrangement of it we are indebted to Mr. Stevens.

The question naturally arises, " To what age do these monuments belong ? " " When and by whom were Stonehenge and Abury erected ? " As regards the latter, history is entirely silent. Stonehenge, with the exception possibly of an allusion in Hecatæus, is unmentioned by any Greek or Roman writer ; nor is there any reference to it in Gildas, Nennius, Bede, or in the Saxon Chronicle. Henry of Huntingdon, in the twelfth century, alludes to it with admiration, but expresses no opinion as to its date or origin.

In the same century, Geoffrey of Monmouth, who, in the words of Dr. Guest, " is everywhere found darkening the pure light of our early history," gave to the world that which some call an historical account of Stonehenge, namely, that it was erected in the fifth century, to commemorate the treacherous murder of the British by Hengist.

The stones are said to have come from Africa, whence they were transported by giants to the plains of Kildare ; and from thence, by the enchantments of Merlin, carried to Salisbury Plain. The question has been well discussed by one of our members, Mr. Long, in his recent work on *Stonehenge and its Barrows* in which he has usefully brought together our present information on the subject; and I will therefore only add that, for my own part, I look upon the account given by Geoffrey as altogether mythical.

It is remarkable that the source of the small inner stones, which, as Stukely first pointed out, are of a different material from the others, is still uncertain,[1] but the large ones are certainly "Sarcen" stones, such as are still shown in many places on the Plain. The best evidence as to the age of Stonehenge seems to me derivable from the contents of the tumuli surrounding it. Within a radius of three miles round Stonehenge there are no less than 300 tumuli; which is, I need not say, a much larger number than are found anywhere else within an equal area. We can hardly doubt, I think, that these tumuli cluster round the great monument; or, at least, that the same circumstances which induced the erection of Stonehenge on its present site, led also, either directly or indirectly, to the remarkable assemblage of tumuli round it. Now, 250 of these tumuli were opened by our great Antiquary, Sir Richard Colt Hoare, and are described in his *Ancient Wiltshire* If these belonged to the post Roman period, we should naturally expect to find iron weapons, and, especially knives, coins,

---

[1] There are, in fact, four kinds of stones in Stonehenge. The great outer circle and the trilithons are "Sarcen" stones, that is to say, they are formed from the sandstone blocks of the neighbourhood. The majority of the small pillars forming the inner circle consist of an igneous rock known as Diabase, but four stones of this series are schistoid, and resemble some of the Silurian and Cambrian rocks of North Wales and Cumberland. Lastly, the so-called altar-stone is grey sandstone, resembling some of the Devonian and Cambrian rocks.—Maskelyne, *Wilts. Arch. and Nat. Hist. Magazine*, Oct. 1877.

well-burnt pottery, and other relics, characteristic of the
period. Is this so? Not at all. The primary inter-
ment was not in any case accompanied by objects of
iron, while in no less than thirty-nine cases, bronze was
present.

We have then, I think, strong grounds for referring
these monuments to the Bronze Age; and if this be true
of Stonehenge, it probably is the case with Abury also,
which seems decidedly more archaic, the stones, for
instance, being rough, while those of Stonehenge are
hewn.

Now when was the Bronze Age? And what do archæologists mean by the Bronze Age? I ask this question
because, though it has been repeatedly answered, there
is still a great misapprehension even in the minds of
some who have written on the subject.

By the Bronze Age, then, we mean a period when the
weapons were made almost entirely, and ornaments principally, of Bronze; that is to say, of Copper and Tin;
Gold being rare, Iron and Silver still more so, or even
unknown, as was also the case with Coins and Glass.

Some archæologists, indeed, have considered the Bronze
swords and daggers which characterise the Bronze Age
to be really Roman. This question has been much discussed, and I will not now enlarge on it, but will only
say, that in my judgment these arms are not found
with Roman remains, and that the Roman weapons were
made of iron, the word " ferrum " being synonymous with
a sword. On this point, I have taken some pains to
ascertain the opinions of Italian archæologists. Bronze
swords, daggers, &c., occur south of the Alps, the very
patterns being in some places identical with those of

Northern Europe. But I believe it may be asserted that no object characteristic of the Bronze Age has ever been found in a Roman tomb; none have been met with at Pompeii; and those Italian archæologists whom I have been able to consult, all agree that they are undeniably Pre-Roman.

If indeed the Bronze swords and daggers were of Roman origin, they ought to be more numerous in Italy than in the north. Now what are the facts? The museum of the Royal Irish Academy contains no less than 300 swords and daggers of Bronze. As regards other countries, M. Chantre, who has been collecting statistics on the subject, has been good enough to inform me that the French Museums contain 409, those of Sweden (including poniards) 480, and of Denmark 600, while in Italy he knows of 60 only. These numbers seem to me to militate very strongly against the views of those who would ascribe those weapons to the Romans. When, then, was the Bronze Age? We know that Iron was known in the time of Homer, which seems to have been, as regards the South of Europe, the period of transition from the age of Iron to that of Bronze. In the Pentateuch, excluding Deuteronomy (which probably belongs to a much later date) Brass, that is to say Bronze, is frequently mentioned, while Iron is only alluded to four times.

Coins were first struck 7—800 B.C. as some say by the Œginetans under Pheidon, King of Argos, though Herodotus ascribes them to the Lydians.

It is true that the use of iron may have been known in Southern Europe long before it was introduced in the north. On the whole, however, I am disposed to think

that when iron was once discovered, its use would spread
somewhat rapidly ; and the similarity of form, of pattern,
and of ornaments existing between the Bronze arms and
implements throughout Europe, seems to negative the
idea that Bronze was in use for such purposes in the
north for any great length of time after it had been
replaced by Iron in the south.

It is, however, more than likely that many of our
smaller Wiltshire tumuli belong to a still earlier period,
namely, to the Neolithic, or later Stone Age, though it
is not easy to say which of them do so. This is probably also the case with the large chambered tumuli, in
which as yet no metal has been discovered. As regards
the Stone Age, the same word of caution is as necessary
as in that of Bronze. There have been some who denied
the very existence of such a period, alleging generally as
their reason against this proposed classification that implements and weapons of stone were used in conjunction
with those of metal. This, however, no one denies.
The characteristic of the Stone Age is not the presence of stone, but the absence of metal ; and if the
name were to be a definition, the period would be more
correctly designated as non-metallic. That there was
indeed a time when stone axes, knives and javelin
heads were used in Europe, and when metal was unknown,
cannot I think be for a moment doubted or denied by
any one who has carefully looked into the evidence.
These objects of stone, so well described by Mr. Evans
in his excellent work on the Ancient Stone Implements
of Great Britain are of the most varied character ; mere
flakes used as knives, scrapers for preparing skins, axes,
adzes, hammers, gouges, chisels, arrowheads, javelin

heads, swords, picks, awls, slingstones and many other forms; these, too, found not singly or in small numbers but by hundreds and thousands, I might say tens of thousands, attest the important part which has been played by stone in the early stages of the development of the human race. For our knowledge of this period we are mainly indebted, firstly, to the shell mounds or refuse heaps of Denmark so well studied by Steenstrup and Wörsaae; secondly, to the tumuli or burial mounds; thirdly, to the remains found in caves; and fourthly, to the Swiss lake dwellings, first made known to us by Keller, and afterwards studied with so much zeal and ability by Morlot, Troyon, Desor, Schwab and other Swiss archæologists.

From these sources we get some idea of the conditions of life existing during the Stone Age.

The use of pottery was known, but the potter's wheel does not seem to have been as yet discovered. Man was clothed in skins, but partly also, in all probability, in garments made of flax. His food was derived principally from animals killed in the chase, but he had probably domesticated the ox as well as the goat, the pig and the dog, nor was he altogether ignorant of agriculture. Traces of dwellings of this period have been found in various parts of England; and in this county, the circular depressions which occur frequently on the Downs, generally collected in groups, are of this character. The dwellings consisted of pits sunk into the ground, and probably covered by a roof consisting of branches of trees, over which again a coating of turf and earth may probably have been placed. The Swiss lake dwellings of this period were constructed

on platforms supported on piles driven into the muddy
bottom of the lakes, and in some cases still further
supported by having stones heaped up round them.   In
one case a large canoe has been met with, evidently
wrecked while on its way to one of the lake settlements, loaded with a freight of such stones. It must
be admitted indeed that our knowledge of the Stone
Age is still scanty, fragmentary, and unsatisfactory ; on
the other hand, the stone weapons and implements found
in Europe so very closely resemble those in use amongst
various races of existing savages that they give us vivid,
and I think to a great extent, accurate ideas of the mode
of life which prevailed at that distant period ; distant
indeed it was, according to the ideas of chronology which
almost universally prevailed until within the last quarter
of a century, for we can scarcely doubt that even the
later Stone Age goes back to a period more remote than
the 6,000 years which were traditionally supposed to be
the limit of man's existence on earth.   No doubt, indeed,
the difficulties of the received chronology had long been
felt.   Well-marked varieties of the human race are
shown by the Egyptian monuments to have existed as
early, at any rate, as the fifteenth century before Christ.
The antiquity of Man is also indicated by the differences
of language, and by the existence of powerful and
flourishing monarchs at a very early period ; for the
pyramids themselves were constructed about 4,000 years
B.C., and even at that early period it would appear that
the Sphinx was suffering from age, for we possess a
decree by which Cheops provided for its repair.

Quitting now the Neolithic, or second Stone Age, we
come to the Palæolithic or first Stone Age.   At this

period man appears to have been ignorant not only of metals, but of pottery. The stone implements are much ruder, and are simply chipped into form, being never ground or polished. We have no evidence of the existence of any domestic animals, and man probably lived mainly on the produce of the chase, contending for the possession of Europe with animals which now exist only in distant regions, or have become entirely extinct. So unexpected were these facts, so improbable did they appear, that geologists accepted them only after reiterated and incontrovertible proofs. The researches of MM. Tournal and Christol in the caves of the south of France, now just half a century ago—the still more complete investigations of Dr. Schmerling in those of Belgium, during the years 1833-34—scarcely raised even a doubt upon the subject. Those of Mr. McEnery in Kent's Cavern attracted little attention; subsequent observations made there by Mr. Vivian were refused publication, on account of the inherent improbability of the conclusions to which they pointed. The discoveries of M. Boucher de Perthes were neglected for a quarter of a century, and it is not too much to say that if geologists are open to blame at all for their behaviour with reference to this question, it would certainly be rather for their incredulity—for their blind adherence to traditional chronology—than for too ready an acceptance of new views. Yet they may well be pardoned for long hesitation before they could bring themselves to believe that man really inhabited Europe at a time when not only the urus and the bison and the reindeer occupied the whole of Europe as far south as the Alps, but when the cave lion, the cave bear, the long-haired rhinoceros, the mammoth, the musk sheep, and the hippopotamus also formed part of the European fauna; when the climate was very different and liable to great oscillations; when our rivers had but begun to excavate their valleys, and the whole condition of the country must therefore have been singularly different from what it is now. Gradually, however, the evidence became overwhelming: the statements of Tournal and Christol were confirmed by Lartet and Christy, by De Vibraye and others; those of Schmerling by Dupont; of McEnery by Vivian and Pengelly; and at length the evidence, well summed up in his work on *Cave Hunting*, by Mr. Boyd Dawkins, himself a successful worker in this field of research, left no room for doubt. As regards the Drift Gravels, M. de Perthes not only discovered unmistakable flint implements in the drift gravel of the Somme valley, but he convinced every one that these implements really belonged to the gravels in which they occurred, and he taught us to find similar implements for ourselves in the corresponding strata of the river systems. For the full significance, however, of these facts, we are indebted to the profound geological knowledge of Mr. Prestwich; while Mr. Evans taught us to appreciate the essential characteristics which distinguish the stone implements of the two periods, to which I have ventured to give the names Palæolithic and Neolithic.

Characteristic remains of the Palæolithic period have been found in this neighbourhood by Dr. Blackmore, Mr. Stevens, Mr. James Brown, and others. We shall see an interesting series of them when we visit the Museum.

Whether man existed in Europe at a still earlier period, in preglacial, or even, as some suppose, in miocene times, is a question still under discussion, into which I will not now enter. Under any circumstances, the antiquity of the human race must be very considerable.

This conclusion rests upon three distinct considerations. The forms of the implements are indeed unlike those which characterise the Neolithic period. But although it is a remarkable fact, and one the significance of which must not be overlooked, that while on the one hand, the forms of the Palæolithic period are entirely wanting in our tumuli; so on the other, the polished implements, the finely carved spearheads of the Neolithic period, have never yet been found in the drift gravel. Nevertheless, their antiquity does not depend on these considerations. The three reasons which have induced geologists and antiquaries to ascribe so great an age to these remains are—firstly, the mammalian relics with which they are associated; secondly, and still more, the nature and position of the deposits in which they occur; lastly, and most of all, the changes of climate which are indicated by the facts. The animal remains which characterise this period are certainly of very great interest. Who would have thought, not many years ago, that the remarkable fauna to which I have just alluded had ever inhabited our valleys, wandered in our forests and over our downs.

A striking illustration of this fauna is that discovered in the Cave of Kesserloch, near Thayngen, in Switzerland, recently explored by Mr. Merk, whose memoir has been translated into English by Mr. Lee.

Not only, however, is this fauna remarkable from the list of species, but also with reference to their relative abundance. Thus, the Alpine and the field hare were both present, but the former was by far the most abundant. The reindeer, again, was fifty times as numerous as the red deer; but, perhaps, the most surprising case is that of the foxes. About eighty individuals were represented, and of these more than forty-five belonged to the *Canis fulvus*, or North American fox; more than twenty to the Arctic fox (*Canis lagopus*), which has also been met with in England by Mr. Busk under similar circumstances, and will, probably, be found to have been sometimes mistaken for the common fox; while of the common European fox, only two or three could be determined. In other respects, the fauna of this ancient period is interesting, as tending to connect forms now distinct. Thus, according to Mr. Busk, than whom there is no higher authority on the Pleistocene mammalia, some remains of bears found in the bone caves are identical with those of the American grizzly bear; and the ancient bison was intermediate between the existing bison of America and the European aurochs.

The next consideration on which the antiquity of these remains depends, is the nature and position of the river gravels in which they are found. These gravels have evidently been formed and deposited by the rivers themselves, when they ran at a higher level, that is to say, before they had excavated their valleys to the present depth. Even at that time, the areas of drainage, at least of the principal rivers in question, for instance the Somme, the Seine, the Oise, the Thames, &c., were the same as now. This is proved by the fact that the pebbles which constitute the gravels are always such as might have been derived from the area of drainage. Thus the gravels of the Somme are made up of flint pebbles, the

district drained by that river being entirely a chalk area.
But if the river during the Palæolithic period had extended only six miles further inland, it would have
entered upon an area containing rocks of earlier periods,
fragments of which must in such a case have formed a
constituent part of its gravels.   This consideration is
very important, because it shows that the valleys must
have been excavated by the present rivers; even ad-
mitting that from the then condition of the climate, and
from other considerations floods of that period may have
been both more frequent and more violent.   Still the
excavation of the valleys must have been due to the
rainfall of each respective area, and thus not ascribable
either to one great cataclysm or to the fact of the
rivers having drained larger areas than at present.   In
many cases, the excavation of the valley is even greater
than might at first be supposed.   The valley of the
Somme, for instance, is forty feet deeper in reality than
its present form would indicate, the river having filled it
up again to that extent.

The valley itself is from 200 to 250 feet in depth, and
although this affords us no means of making even an
approximate calculation as to time, still it is obvious that
to excavate a valley, such as that of the Somme, to a
depth of 250 feet, and to fill it up to the extent of thirty
or forty feet with sand, silt and peat, must have required
a very considerable lapse of time.

Passing on now to the question of climate, it will be
observed that the assemblage of mammalia to which I
have already referred, is remarkable in several ways.   It
is interesting to find that man coexisted in our woods
and valleys—on Salisbury Plain, and on the banks of the

Avon—with animals which are now to be found only in remote regions, or which are altogether extinct. It is sufficiently surprising to reflect that on this very spot where we are now assembled there once ranged large herds of those strange and gigantic animals ; but another most interesting consideration is, that when we come to consider them more closely, we shall find that they constitute in reality two distinct groups. The hippopotamus, for instance, and probably the hyena, extended into Great Britain, the porcupine into Belgium, the African elephant into Spain and Sicily ; facts all indicating a climate warmer than the present. On the other hand, the mammoth and the long-haired rhinoceros, the reindeer and the marmot, the arctic hare and fox, the ibex, chamois, and the musk-sheep, point decidedly to arctic conditions. The musk-sheep indeed has the most northern range of any known mammal.

Passing over for the present those mammalia which seem to indicate a tropical climate, let us consider what may be called the arctic group, and I may observe in passing that the existence of a very cold climate during the latest geological period had been inferred from other considerations, even when our knowledge of the mammalian fauna was much less considerable and consequently less suggestive. Various theories have been suggested to account for the fact that at a period, geologically speaking so recent, the climate of Europe should have been so different from what it is at present, and the best authorities seem now to consider that the true explanation is to be found in astronomical causes. If the plane of the equator coincided exactly with that of the ecliptic, every day would be succeeded by a night of equal length.

In consequence, however, of the obliquity of the ecliptic,
this only happens twice in the year, namely, on the 20th
of March and 23rd of September, which days divide the
year into two halves, the day being longer than the night
in the spring and summer, and shorter, on the other
hand, in autumn and winter.   Under existing circumstances then, we have in the northern hemisphere seven
days more of summer than of winter, while in the southern
hemisphere they have, on the other hand, seven days
more of winter than of summer.   This, however, has not
been, nor will it be always the case ; on the contrary, a
gradual change is continually taking place, during a cycle
of 21,000 years.   Taken by itself, the balance of astronomical authority is not, I think, of opinion that this
would greatly influence our climate.   The effect, however,
which the obliquity of the ecliptic would exercise depends
greatly on the degree of eccentricity of the earth's orbit.
This is continually changing, and the more elliptical it is,
the greater is the effect produced by the above mentioned
causes.   At present the orbit is nearly circular, and consequently the difference of temperature between the two
hemispheres is less than usual.

Mr. Croll and Mr. Stone have calculated the eccentricity for the last million of years and have shown that
there are two periods especially, one namely from 850,000
to 750,000 years ago, the other from 200,000 to 100,000
years ago, when the eccentricity of the orbit was far
greater than usual, and when, therefore, the difference
of temperature between the two hemispheres must also
have been unusually great.   From 100,000 to 200,000
years ago, then, there was a period when our climate
underwent violent oscillations, being for 10,500 years

far colder than now, then for a similar period far hotter, then far colder again, and so on for several variations. These alternations of hot and cold periods beautifully explain the difficult problem of how to account for the existence of remains belonging to tropical and to arctic animals, associated together in the same river gravels. It also throws light on the fact, first pointed out by my friend M. Morlot, that there are in Switzerland geological indications of several periods of extreme cold, with others of more genial climate, and Mr. Croll in his *Climate and Time*, has pointed out, from the evidence of 250 borings in the Scotch glacial beds, that many of them show evidence of the existence of warm interglacial periods.

The antiquity of this period, therefore, really must be solved by the mathematician and physicist, rather than by the antiquary, and it affords us an excellent illustration of the manner in which the different branches of science depend upon one another, and of the fact that the more science advances, the more necessary it is that our higher education should be based on a wide foundation.

DESCRIPTION OF ILLUSTRATIONS

Plate, Figure.	Place of Issue.	Date.	Description of Obverse.
I. A	China . . .	1st century A.D. The usurper Wang Mang	Legend, Pu-ho (Shirt of Commerce)
B	China . . .	4th or 3rd century B.C. Tse dynasty	Legend, Tseih-mih-Taou (Knife of the Tseih-mih city or fief) . .
I. 1	Lydia . . .	7th century B.C. .	Oblong incuse between square incuses ; no device . . . . .
2	Aegina .	6th century B.C. .	Sea-tortoise. . . . .
3	Persia . . .	5th century B.C. .	The king kneeling ; holds bow and javelin . . . .
4	Sidon . . .	4th century B.C. About the time of Strato . . .	The king in his chariot ; below, a ram, *incuse* . . . . .
5	Syracuse . .	Early in the 4th century ; time of Dionysius I. . .	ΣΥΡΑΚΟΣΙΩΝ. Head of Persephone amid dolphins ; below ΕΥΑΙΝΕ[ΤΟΣ], engraver's name . . . .
6	Metapontum in Italy .	Early in the 4th century . . .	Head of Persephone (Proserpine).
II. 1	Amphipelis in Macedon .	Philip II., B.C. 359–336	Head of Apollo, laureate . . .
3	S.E. Britain .		Types copied from No. 1, except for the spike behind the ear, which may come from the Head of Persephone on Sicilian or Carthaginian Coins (cf. Plate I., 5 and 6) . . . .
4	S.E. Britain .	1st century B.C. .	
5	S. coast of Britain . .		
6	Camulodunum in Britain .	Cunobelin, died A.D. 40–43	CVNO. Horse galloping ; above a branch . . . .
2	Thrace . . .	Lysimachus, died B.C. 281 . . .	Head of Alexander the Great wearing diadem and horn of Ammon . . . , . . .
7	Judæa . . .	Simon the Maccabee, B.C. 144–135	Hebrew Inscription :—Shekel of Israel, year 4. A chalice . .
8	Ascalon in Judæa . .	Cleopatra of Egypt, B.C. 50. . . .	Head of the Queen, wearing diadem . . . .
9	Rome . . .	Augustus, in memory of his uncle, killed B.C. 44 .	C . CAESAR . DICT . PERP . PONT . MAX. (Caius Caesar, Dictator Perpetuus, Pontifex Maximus.) Head of Julius Caesar
10	Rome . . .	Antoninus Pius, A.D. 138–161 .	ANTONINVS AVG. PIVS P.P. TR . P . COS . III. (Antoninus Augustus Pius, Pater Patriae, Tribunicia Potestate, Consul Ter) Head of the Emperor, laureate .

* I am much indebted to Mr. GARDNER, of the British

Description of Reverse.	Remarks.
Plain	Coin fashioned to represent a shirt.
Plain	Coin fashioned to represent a knife.
Marks of anvil	One of the earliest coins extant.
Incuse divided into five	The tortoise was the symbol of the Phœnician goddess of trade.
Rude incuse	These coins were issued, with slight variation, from the time of Darius Hystaspis to the end of the Persian Empire.
A gallery before a fortress ; below, two lions	The fortress probably represents Sidon itself.
Quadriga driven by the City, who is crowned by Victory ; below, the ΑΘΛΑ, armour for prizes	The chariot-type in Sicily alludes to victories with chariots in the Olympic games.
META. Ear of corn with leaf; on leaf, mouse ; in field Φ, for magistrate's name	The types refer to the plenteous harvests of the city.
ΦΙΛΙΠΠΟΥ. Biga ; below, trident (mintmark)	Prototype of Pannonian, British and Gaulish coins.
Types copied from last	These types spread from tribe to tribe, and crossed over from Gaul to Britain.
CAMV. Ear of bearded corn . . .	This is also a copy of Philip's coin ; the horse representing the biga, and the ear of corn the wreath of Apollo.
ΒΑΣΙΛΕΩΣ ΛΥΣΙΜΑΧΟΥ. Pallas seated, holding Victory, monograms in field . .	
Hebrew inscription :—Jerusalem the Holy. Triple lily	Some numismatists give these pieces to the time of Ezra.
ΑΣΚΑΛΩΝΙΤΩΝ ΤΗΣ ΙΕΡΑΣ ΚΑΙ ΑΣΥΛΟΥ. Eagle holding a palm; in the field a monogram, a lesser eagle, and the date LNE (year 55 of the era of Ascalon)	When this coin was struck, Cleopatra was nineteen years of age.
C . CAESAR · COS · PONT · AVG. (Caius Caesar Consul, Pontifex, Augustus. Head of Augustus . .	These Roman aurei formed the gold currency of the world.
BRITANNIA. Figure of Roman Britain, seated, holding military standard	The prototype of our modern penny.

ANCIENT COINS,
PLATE I.

ANCIENT COINS,

PLATE II.

LECTURE VII.

THE INAUGURAL ADDRESS OF THE PRESIDENT,
SIR JOHN LUBBOCK, BART., M.P., F.R.S.

[Read before the Bankers' Institute, 22nd May, 1879.]

ALLOW me to congratulate you, gentlemen, upon the great success which has attended your efforts to found this Institution, which now numbers more than 1,300 members, besides a considerable number of applicants not yet elected. The object of the Institute is, as you are aware, to facilitate the consideration and discussion of matters of interest to the profession, and to afford opportunities for acquisition of a knowledge of the theory of banking. It will arrange meetings for the reading, discussion, and publication of approved papers on subjects connected with commerce and banking, for courses of lectures on mercantile law, political economy, banking, and other kindred subjects. It will probably institute examinations and grant certificates, and will eventually found a library of works on commerce, finance, and political economy. I must confess that, when you did me the honour of requesting me to become your president, I felt some scruples in accepting the invitation, gratifying as it was, on these two grounds —firstly, because my time was already so much occupied,

and, secondly, because I thought you might find so good
a president in our excellent treasurer, Mr. Martin, to
whose efforts the Institute owes so much of its success,
and who represents a firm which happily combines with
the interest of an ancient monument the vigour and
utility of a living institution.   The first duty which
devolves upon your president is to take the chair at the
present meeting, and your committee have expressed a
wish that I should commence by giving an inaugural
address.   On future occasions we shall probably be
occupied very much with practical and economical
questions.   As regards the former, I hope that the
Institute may assist in securing uniformity of action, and
in exercising a judicious influence on custom, which to
so great an extent forms the basis of law.   To-night, for
instance, we are honoured by the presence of a great
authority on banking, Mr. Thomson Hankey, who will
be good enough to give us his views on audits and
balance-sheets.   At the next meeting, Mr. Palgrave, of
the *Economist*, has promised to give us a paper on the
Bank of England, the Bank of France, and the Bank of
Germany.   Nor shall we, I hope, neglect the principles
of political economy, for I believe you will most of you
agree with me when I say that far more money is lost in
business through errors of judgment than through fraud.
It is a national misfortune that political economy is so
completely ignored in our schools.   On the present
occasion, however, I have thought that it might not be
altogether an unfitting prelude to our labours if I
endeavour to trace up the stages by which we have
arrived at the present state of things, dwelling principally on the earlier stages, because the later ones will

doubtless come frequently before us. Unfortunately, when I endeavoured to compress the subject within reasonable limits, I found I could do no more than attempt a very slight and imperfect sketch.

As in so many other matters, the most ancient records of money carry us away to the other side of the world— to the great empire of China. The early history of Chinese currency is principally known to us through a treatise, *Wen-hien t'ung K'ao* ; or, *The Examination of Currency*, by Ma-twan-lin, a great Chinese scholar, who was born about 1245, though his work was not published until 1321. In uncivilized times various objects have served as a standard of value. In the Hudson's Bay territory beavers' skins have long been used in this manner. In ancient Europe cattle were the usual medium of exchange, whence, as every one knows, the word *pecunia*. In the *Zendavesta* the payment of physicians is calculated in the same way, but comparatively few perhaps realize that when we pay our *fee* we are doing the same thing, for the word *fee* is the old word *vieh*, which, as we know, in German still retains the sense of cattle. In Africa and the East Indies shells are, and long have been, used for the same purpose. We even find indications that shells once served as money in China, because as M. Biot, in his interesting memoir on Chinese currency, has pointed out, the words denoting buying, selling, riches, goods, stores, property, prices, cheap, dear, and many others referring to money and wealth, contain the ideographic sign denoting the word *shell*. Indeed, Wangmang, who usurped the Imperial throne about 14 A.D., wishing to return to the ancient state of things, attempted, among other changes, to bring into circulation five different varieties of shells of an arbitrary value.

A curious illustration of the passage from a state of barter to the use of money is found in the fact that pieces of cloth, and knives having been used as in some measure a standard of value, almost as grey shirting is even now, so the earliest Chinese coins were made to resemble pieces of cloth or knives, and there are two principal kinds of coins—the *pu* coins, roughly representing a shirt (Fig. A., Plate I.), and the *tao* coins (Fig. B., Plate I.), which are in the form of a knife. These curious coins have been supposed to go back four thousand one hundred years, and to have been made in the year 2250 B.C. I believe, however, that there is still much doubt on this point. Scimitar-shaped coins also at one time circulated (if I may use the expression) in Persia. But these forms were of course very inconvenient, and the Chinese soon arrived at the opinion that money, which was intended "to roll round the world" should be itself round. A curious feature of Chinese coins, the nail-mark, appears to have originated in an accident very characteristic of China. In the time of Queen Wentek, a model in wax of a proposed coin was brought for her majesty's inspection. In taking hold of it she left on it the impression of one of her nails, and the impression has in consequence not only been a marked characteristic of Chinese coins for hundreds of years, but has even been copied on those of Japan and Corea. The Chinese coins were not struck, as ours are, but cast, which offers peculiar facilities for forging. The history of Chinese coinage, to use Mr. Jevons's words, "is little more than a monstrous repetition of depreciated issues, both public and private, varied by occasional meritorious but often unsuccessful efforts to restore the standard of currency." Mr. Vissering gives us several interesting illustrations of the financial discussions of the Chinese. " As to the desire of your majesty," for instance, says Lutui, " to cast money and to arrange the currency in order to repair its present vicious state, it is just the same as if you would rear a fish in a caldron of boiling water, or roost a bird on a hot fire. Water and wood are essential for the life of fish and birds. But in using them in the wrong way you will surely cause the bird to be scorched and the fish to be cooked to shreds."

Not only did the Chinese possess coins at a very early period, but they were also the inventors of bank notes. Some writers regard bank notes as having originated about 119 B.C., in the reign of the Emperor Ou-ti. At this time the court was in want of money, and to raise it Klaproth tells us that the prime minister hit upon the following device :—When any princes or courtiers entered the imperial presence, it was customary to cover the face with a piece of skin. It was first decreed then, that for this purpose the skin of certain white deer kept in one of the royal parks should alone be permitted, and then these pieces of skin were sold for a high price. But although they appear to have passed from one noble to another, they do not seem ever to have entered into general circulation. It was therefore very different from the Russian skin money. In this case, the notes were " used instead of the skins from which they were cut, the skins themselves being too bulky and heavy to be constantly carried backward and forward. Only a little piece was cut off to figure as a token of possession of

the whole skin. The ownership was proved when the
piece fitted in the hole." True bank notes are said to
have been invented about 800 A.D., in the reign of Hian-
tsoung, of the dynasty of Thang, and were called
feytsien, or flying money. It is curious, however, though
not surprising, to find that the temptation to over issue
led to the same results in China as in the West. The
value of the notes fell, until at length it took 11,000
min., or £3,000 nominal, to buy a cake of rice, and the
use of notes appears to have been abandoned. Subsequently the issue was revived, and Tchang-yang (960—
990 A.D.) seems to have been the first private person
who issued notes. Somewhat later, under the Emperor
Tching-tsong (997—1022), this invention was largely
extended. Sixteen of the richest firms united to form
a bank of issue, which emitted paper money in series,
some payable every three years.

The earliest mention in European literature of paper,
or rather cotton, money appears to be by Rubruquis, a
monk, who was sent by St. Louis, in the year 1252, to
the court of the Mongol Prince Mangu-Khan, but he
merely mentions the fact of its existence. Marco Polo,
who resided from 1275 to 1284 at the court of Kublai-
Khan,—I do not know whether in

> " the stately pleasure dome
> Where Alph, the sacred river, ran
> Through caverns measureless to man
> Down to a sunless sea,"—

gives us a longer and interesting account of the note
system, which he greatly admired, and he concludes by
saying, " Now you have heard the ways and means

whereby the great Khan may have, and, in fact, has, more treasure than all the kings in the world. You know all about it, and the reason why." But this apparent facility of creating money led, in the East, as it has elsewhere, to great abuses. Sir John Mandeville, who was in Tartary shortly afterwards, in 1322, tells us that the " Emperour may dispenden als moche as he wile withouten estymacioum. For he despendeth not, he maketh no money, but of lether emprented, or of papyre. . . . For there and beyonde hem'thei make no money, nouther of gold nor of sylver. And therefore he may despende ynow and outrageously." The Great Khan seems to have been himself of the same opinion. He appears to have " despent outrageously," and the value of the paper money again fell to a very small fraction of its nominal amount, causing great discontent and misery, until about the middle of the sixteenth century, under the Mandchu dynasty, it was abolished, and appears to have been so completely forgotten, that the Jesuit father, Gabriel de Magaillans, who resided at Pekin about 1668, observes that there is no recollection of paper money having ever existed in the manner described by Marco Polo; though two centuries later it was again in use. It must be observed, however, that these Chinese bank notes differed from ours in one essential, namely, they were not payable at sight. Western notes, even when not payable at all, have generally purported to be exchangeable at the will of the holder, but this principle the Chinese did not adopt, and their notes were only payable at certain specified periods.

Various savage races are, we know, in the habit of burying with the dead his wives, slaves, or other possessions. So also in Greece, it was usual to place a piece of money in the mouth of the deceased, as Charon's fee.

In China also paper money is said to have been similarly treated. It was, we are informed, sometimes burnt at funerals in order that the dead might have some ready money to start with in the world of spirits. At the same time, in finance, as in many other matters, the Chinese, though. they anticipated the white races, have not advanced so far. Their system of currency is still archaic, and banking appears to be but little developed. Deposits, which constitute the life-blood of banking, are, we are told, exceptional. Bills circulate, or are bought and sold at the exchanges in Pekin and other cities, but Chinese banking seems almost to confine itself to issuing and repaying bills. Moreover, though the Chinese possess, and have so long possessed a coinage, it is only suitable to small payments, and in all large transactions ingots are extensively used. These ingots have no public stamp, although they often bear the mark of the maker, which is sometimes so well known that a verification is dispensed with.

In their financial and banking arrangements, the Japanese seem to have been much behind the Chinese. They had, indeed, a form of paper money. The Daimios, or feudal lords, in various districts, issued little cards representing very small values. In the museum of Leyden is one of these issued in 1688. The bank notes, however, never reached a high state of development, and in the 59th volume of the great *Encyclopædia San-tsai-dyn*, the subject is—I quote from Vissering—thus contemptuously dismissed : " Under the reign of the Sung and Yuen dynasties paper money was made use of. It was uncommonly inconvenient. When in the rain it got soaked and the mice gnawed at it, it became as if one possessed a raven. When carried in the breast pocket or the money belt, the consequence was that it was destroyed by abrasion."

Money seems to us now so obvious a convenience, and so much a necessity of commerce, that it appears almost inconceivable that a people who created the Sphinx and the Pyramids, the temples of Ipsamboul and Karnac, should have been entirely ignorant of coins. Yet it appears from the statements of Herodotus, and the evidence of the monuments themselves, that this was really the case. As regards the commercial and banking systems of ancient Egypt, we are almost entirely without information. Their standard of value seems to have been the " outen " or " ten " of copper (94-96 grammes), which circulated like the æs rude of the Romans by weight, and ·in the form of bricks, being measured by the balance : it was obtained from the mines of Mount Sinai, which were worked as early as the fourth dynasty. Gold and Silver appear to have been also used, though less frequently ; like copper, they were sometimes in the form of bricks, but generally in rings, resembling the ring money of the ancient Celts, which is said to have been employed in Ireland down to the twelfth century, and still holds its own in the interior of Africa. This approximated very nearly to the possession of money, but it wanted what the Roman lawyers called " the law " and " the form." Neither the weight nor the pureness was guaranteed by any public authority. Such a state of things seems to us very inconvenient, but after all it is not very different from that which prevails in China even at the present day. The first money struck in Egypt, and that for the use rather of the Greek and Phœnician merchants than of the natives, was by the Satrap Aryandes.

In ancient Babylonia and Assyria, as in Egypt, the precious metals, and especially silver, circulated as uncoined ingots. They were readily taken, indeed, but taken by weight and verified by the balance like any other merchandize. The excavations in Assyria and Babylon, which have thrown so much light upon ancient history, have afforded us some interesting information as to the commercial arrangements of these countries, and we now possess a considerable number of receipts, contracts, and other records relating to loans of silver on personal securities at fixed rates of interest, loans on landed or house property; sales of land, in one case with a plan; sales of slaves, &c. These were engraved on tablets of clay, which were then burnt. M. Lenormant divides these most interesting documents into five principal types:—1. Simple obligations. 2. Obligations with a penal clause in case of non-fulfilment. One he gives which had seventy-nine days to run. 3. Obligations with the guarantee of a third party. 4. Obligations payable to a third person. 5. Drafts drawn upon one place, payable in another. I may give the following illustrations of these letters of credit from two specimens in my collection, kindly read for me by Mr. Pinches. 1. "Loan of two-thirds of a mana of coined silver by Nabu-sum-ikum to Bainsat, at an interest of one shekel monthly upon the mana; fourth day of Sivan, eighth year of

Darius ; " and a second—" Loan of five mana of silver by
Nabu-zer-iddin to Belnasir. The money to be repaid in
instalments of a shekel and a half, beginning in Nisan,
fifteenth day of Tebet, thirty-fourth year of Nebu-
chadnezzar." The Assyrian drafts appear to have been
negotiable but from the nature of things could not pass
by endorsement, because when the clay was once baked
nothing new could be added, and under these circumstances
the name of the payee was frequently omitted. It seems
to follow that they must have been regularly advised.
It is certainly remarkable that such instruments, and
especially letters of credit, should have preceded the use
of coins. The earliest banking firm of which we have
any account is said to be that of Egibi & Company, for
our knowledge of whom we are indebted to Mr. Bos-
cawen, Mr. Pinches, and Mr. Hilton Price. Several
documents and records belonging to this family are in
the British Museum. They are on clay tablets, and
were discovered in an earthenware jar, found in the
neighbourhood of Hillah, a few miles from Babylon.
The house is said to have acted as a sort of national
bank of Babylon ; the founder of the house, Egibi,
probably lived in the reign of Sennacherib, about 700
B.C. This family has been traced during a century and
a half, and through five generations, down to the reign
of Darius. At the same time, the tablets hitherto translated scarcely seem to me to prove that the firm [1] acted
as bankers, in our sense of the word.

As regards the Hebrews, Mr. Poole tells us there is no

[1] I am much indebted to Mr. Poole, Mr. Head, Mr. Gardner, and
Mr. Evans for the information which they have kindly given me on
various points connected with the history of money.

distinct allusion to coined money in the books of the Old Testament, before the return from Babylon. Shekels, of course, are often mentioned, but the word, like our pound, denotes a weight as well as a coin, and in the older Scriptures it appears to have been used in the former sense. The earliest distinct mention of coins in the Bible is supposed to refer to Persian money, the word "drachm," which appears in our version, being a mistake for "daric." These "darics" have on the obverse the king kneeling, holding a bow and arrow. The reverse shows a rude incuse. They were probably struck in the fifth century B.C. (Fig. III., Plate I.). At a much earlier date, indeed, we read that Abimelech gave Abraham "a thousand pieces of silver" in expiation of his treatment of Sarah ; and, again, that Joseph was sold to the Ishmaelites for "twenty pieces of silver." But in both these cases it will be observed that the word "pieces" is in italics, and there is much doubt about the word : in the Septuagint it is "shekels." Considering the zeal and success with which the Jewish race subsequently devoted themselves to commerce and finance, it is remarkable how small a part these professions play in the early history of the race. One ingenious writer indeed has attempted to account for the turbulence and frowardness of the Jews in ancient times by suggesting that they were fretted, being driven by circumstances into pastoral and agricultural pursuits against all their instinctive and natural tendencies, being, in fact, "*des banquiers comprimés.*" One type of the ancient shekels (Fig. VII., Plate II.) has on the obverse, in Hebrew, "Shekel of Israel, year 4," above a chalice. On the reverse, "Jerusalem, the Holy," and a triple lily. Some

numismatists ascribe these coins to Ezra. The first
Jewish coins were apparently struck by Simon the
Maccabee, under a grant from Antiochus the Seventh.

The earliest coinage in the Western world is generally
ascribed to Pheidon, king of Argos and Ægina, who has
also the great merit of having introduced the use of
weights and measures. According to Herodotus, however, we owe this invention of money to the Lydians,
probably in the reign of Gyges, about 700 B.C. The
question turns very much on the date of Pheidon, in
reference to which there is great uncertainty. Some
writers have carried him back to 895 B.C., which seems
to be certainly untenable, while others have endeavoured
to bring his date down to 660 B.C. The claims of the
Lydians have recently been advocated by some eminent
authorities, especially Rawlinson, Barclay Head, and
Lenormant. Lord Liverpool also, in deference to the
authority of Herodotus, inclined to the same opinion.
In either case the honour rests with the Greek race.
The early coins form an interesting transition between
the metallic ingots which previously performed the
functions of currency and true money. Those of Lydia
(Fig. I., Plate I.) are not round, but oval, with an official
stamp indicating their weight and giving their legal
value : the Æginetan silver staters also imitate the
elongated form of the earlier period, and are even more
irregular than those of Lydia. Still they possess more
of the character of a true coinage, in having been struck
on a block. In the following illustrations of ancient
coins, a silver coin (Fig. II., Plate II.) in the British
Museum, ascribed to Pheidon, is shown. On the one
side is the incuse square, or punch-mark, and on the

other a tortoise—the symbol of the Phœnician goddess
of the sea and trade.   One of the other figures represents a Lydian coin (Fig. I., Plate I.), and is supposed
to be one of the earliest known.   It is perhaps of the
time of Gyges, but in Mr. Head's opinion certainly not
later than Ardys.   Many of these ancient coins have
been found in the neighbourhood of Sardes.   They have
a device on one side only, the other being occupied by
the incuse square, which is the admitted sign of the
earlier condition of the earliest coins.   "The masses of
metal," says Rawlinson, "prepared for coinage were
originally placed upon an anvil with a rough excrescence
protruding from it, having for its object to catch and
hold the metal while the impression was made by means
of a die placed above and struck with a hammer.   This
excrescence, a mere rude and rough square at first, was
gradually improved, being first divided into compartments and then ornamented with a pattern, until
gradually it became a second device, retaining, however,
to a late date its original square shape.   In the Lydian
coins the quadratum incusum is of the most archaic
type, having neither pattern nor divisions, and present-
ing the appearance which might be produced by the
impression of a broken nail."

The Greek coinage, however rude at first, soon acquired
a beauty and perfection surpassing all our modern efforts.
The staters, for instance, of Philip (Fig. I., Plate II.) and
of Alexander, the coins of Syracuse and Metapontum
(Figs. V. and VI., Plate I.), present to us the most
lovely female faces, and deities—perfect models of
human beauty.   Animals also are admirably represented
—not only the horse, the lion, &c., but other smaller

creatures, as the harvest-mouse on an ear of wheat on a Metapontum coin (Fig. VI., Plate I.), and even insects, as, for instance, the praying-mantis. The heads on the earliest coins represent gods and goddesses, the first human head being that of Alexander the Great on a coin of Lysimachus (Fig. II., Plate II), and even in this case the great Conqueror is represented in his divine character as descended from Jupiter Ammon, which is indicated by the ram's horns. It would not, however, be fair to modern mints to attribute the comparative poverty of modern coins to want of skill. It is a great convenience that coins should lie flatly one on another, and the greater boldness of ancient coins, however it may add to their beauty, necessarily rendered this impossible.

Not only were the Greek coins admirable for their beauty, but they were also made of pure metal and full weight, offering in this respect a striking contrast to those of most other countries. There were, however, of course, exceptions. Thus the money of Phocæa was notorious for its bad quality. Herodotus mentions, though with some doubt, that Polycrates, tyrant of Samos, having to pay a large sum to the Lacedæmonians, " coined a large quantity of the country money in lead, had it gilt, and gave it to them ; and that they, having received it, thereupon took their departure." That the true theory of coinage was well understood in Greece, we may see from the words of Aristotle, who thus describes the origin of coins :—

It became necessary, therefore, to think of certain commodities, easily manageable and safely transportable, and of which the uses are so general and so numerous, that they insured the certainty of always obtaining for them the articles wanted in exchange. The

metals, particularly iron and silver and several others, exactly
correspond to this description. They were employed, therefore,
by general agreement as the ordinary standard of value and the
common measure of exchange, being themselves estimated at first
by their bulk and weight, and afterwards stamped, in order to save
the trouble of measuring and weighing them.

In ancient Greece, as now, the right of coinage was
a prerogative of the sovereign. And here we find a
curious difference between βασιλεύς and the τύραννος.
The former coined in his own name, but the τύραννοι,
however absolute, never did so :[1] their money was issued
in the name of the people.

Coins are, of course, very instructive from an historical
point of view. Nevertheless it is somewhat remarkable
that the Greeks do not seem to have ever struck commemorative medals. Even on their coins they did not
for a long time admit any allusions to contemporary
events, and then only in an indirect manner. Almost
the only exception is the enormous gold piece struck
by Eucratides, king of Bactriana, of which the French
possess the only known example. The fact that it is
just equal to twenty staters, does not prove that it
was ever intended to serve as a coin, against which
its size must have been a great objection. Moreover
it would appear that very few specimens were struck.
Indeed there is some reason to suppose that the French
example is the only one ever made, as the die appears
to have been broken in striking it. Neither the Greeks
nor the Romans had any name for a " medal " as
distinguished from a true coin.

In Greece the original business of bankers seems to
have consisted in changing money for foreigners, but

---

[1] With one exception, Alexander of Pheræ.

they soon commenced banking and allowing interest on deposits. We are incidentally informed that the father of Demosthenes kept part of his fortune with one of these Trapezitæ or bankers. Some of them enjoyed considerable credit. Pasion, for instance, we are told, was well known and trusted all over Greece. The ordinary rates of interest were very high, and will not at all bear comparison with those of the present day, as they ranged from 10 to 37 per cent. ; but the risks also must have been extreme, and notwithstanding this large rate of interest their profits seem to have been small. Even Pasion's business is said to have been worth but £400 a year, which appears scarcely credible. The Greek bankers seem to have been as much notaries as bankers, and a large part of their business consisted in witnessing contracts between others. They seem, however, to have possessed a document not very dissimilar to our cheque. They were acquainted with letters of credit, and had even invented a form of endorsement. Thus Iceratus, we read, drew in Athens a bill on his father in Pontus, which was guaranteed by Pasion, and then bought by Stratocles. Bottomry bonds also were in use. It is often said that the great banks of Greece were the temples, but I confess I have my doubts about this. No doubt they served in some cases as national treasuries, and there are some references in history to deposits being made in the temples, but there is a second and not less important function of banks, viz., repayment of deposits, as to which the evidence is very deficient.

The earliest Roman coins are said to have been struck

either by Numa or by Servius Tullius. They were of
bronze or copper, silver not being used till the first
Punic war, 269 B.C., and gold some sixty years later.
Even under the earlier emperors the different provinces
and colonies had their own coins, and it was not until
the time of Diocletian that one coinage was established
for the whole empire. For a long period, indeed, every
great Roman family had the right of coining denarii with
their own device, though precautions were taken to preclude any tampering with the weight or fineness.

The first step in the degradation of the coinage was
effected by the celebrated Flaminian law. We must,
however, remember that this was passed as a measure
of desperate necessity, when Hannibal was at the gates
of Rome, and when the disasters of Lake Thrasimene
and the Trebia had brought the republic to the very verge
of ruin. By it the denarius was reduced from $\frac{1}{72}$ to $\frac{1}{84}$
of a pound. Still more important in its results was the
principle recognized in the law, namely that the coin
was a " sign." This unfortunate error naturally opened
the door to further debasement. Nevertheless, it was
not till the time of Nero that any further steps were
taken in this direction. He lowered the aureus, and
reduced the denarius from $\frac{1}{84}$ to $\frac{1}{96}$ of a pound, increasing the alloy at the same time from 5 to 10
per cent. After this, though the aureus remained
stationary for some time, the denarius rapidly fell in
value.

Although, as already mentioned, the great Roman
families were long permitted to coin under certain precautions, this was nevertheless not only under the
supervision, but in the name of the state. The first

coins were not inscribed, but afterwards they generally
bore the legend "Roma," not as a geographical expression, but as a recognition of sovereignty. The same
feeling which rendered the Greeks so long reluctant
to put any human head on their coins, influenced
the Romans also : to have done so would have indicated
a claim to sovereignty, which, under a republic, would
of course have been totally inadmissible. During the
earlier period of Roman history, indeed, such coins were
unknown. In the year 58 B.C. M. Æmilius Scaurus
represented himself on a small scale, in the act of
receiving the submission of Aretas, king of the Naba-
theans. We find also Marius, Sylla and Pompey on
their triumphal cars, but not even they ever ventured
to put their likenesses on the coins. This feeling
extended with still greater force to female heads. Even
the representation of the women belonging to the
imperial family under the earliest emperors were not
only posthumous and commemorative, but were moreover at first introduced under the disguise of goddesses.
Thus Julia was represented as Diana. Tiberius, in
honour of his mother Livia, attached her features to
heads of the goddesses Pietas, Justitia and Salus
Augusta. Agrippina was not satisfied with this, and
placed herself on coins with her husband Claudius,
though she did not venture to have one struck with her
own effigy alone. The rule was first broken by Drusus,
who struck coins in honour of his wife Antonia.

The Greeks appear to have introduced banking into
Italy, at least if we may judge from the fact that in
early Latin writers most of the words relating to
banking and finance are of Greek origin, and were

P

gradually replaced by Latin words. The bankers in Rome soon became of great importance, and the old Roman comedies contain many allusions to them, not always, indeed, of a very complimentary description, although their professional honour stood very high. It has been mentioned, as an indication of the unpopularity of Gaulish bankers, that when the revolt of Vercingetorix took place, the houses of the bankers were first attacked. But surely another explanation may be given. Moreover the extortion of high interest was not confined to bankers. Pompey, we are informed, lent money at 50 per cent., Brutus, and Cato himself, at 48 per cent. The rate of interest in Rome, as elsewhere in ancient times, was, in fact, excessive. There was, however, no legal rate till the law of the Twelve Tables. It was then fixed nominally at $8\frac{3}{4}$ per cent. Subsequently, in the time of Cicero, it was raised to 12 per cent., at which it continued until it was reduced by Justinian to 4 per cent. for illustrious persons, for those engaged in commerce 6 per cent., and 8 per cent. in other cases. We are told that all money transactions were carried on through the intervention of bankers, and that they kept the account books of their customers. But, however this may be, the system of banking does not appear to have been very thoroughly developed, because when Cicero sent his son Marcus to complete his education at Athens, he wrote to Atticus to inquire if it would be possible to procure a letter of credit on Athens, or whether it would be necessary for Marcus to carry money with him. The later Roman law contains numerous provisions relating to banks. One is rather curious. It seems that if a banker failed, those who had simply deposited money with him for safety ranked before those who placed sums with him at interest. But although they have been the subject of various learned dissertations, it is by no means clear how the Roman bankers kept their accounts. We may hope that we shall ere long know more about Roman banking, because the house and archives of a Pompeian banker—Lucius Cœcilius Jucundus— have recently been discovered in that city.

By general consent gold, silver and copper have been the metals used as money. Iron, indeed, is said to have been used in Sparta, under the laws of Lycurgus, but in this case there is no reason to suppose that it was ever coined. It seems to have been used as it was, according to Cæsar, amongst the ancient Britons in the form of bars. Pollux mentions that the inhabitants of Byzantium, in ancient times, used iron for coins instead of copper, and so have the Japanese, but on the whole this metal is much too heavy in proportion to its value for convenience. Coins of tin are reported to have been struck by Dionysius of Syracuse, and subsequently in Gaul, under the reigns of Septimius Severus and Caracalla, but they appear to have been almost immediately abandoned again. Cast coins of this metal were in use among the ancient Britons—the similarity of such coins to those of silver constituted a very serious inconvenience. Glass seems to have been likewise, at one time, used for subsidiary coinage in Egypt and in Sicily. Platinum was tried in Russia, but was found unsuitable; lead is still used in Burmah; nickel in Belgium, the United States, Switzerland, and Germany, and in 1869 and 1870 we struck some nickel pence and halfpence for Jamaica. In addition to the commercial uses of coins, they are important from an historical point of view, and also in giving us authentic portraits of many interesting persons—Cæsar, Augustus, Cleopatra,[1] and many others (Figs. VIII., IX., X., Plate II.).

I have already alluded to the high rates of interest which prevailed in former times. These, of course, were very injurious to commerce, and naturally provoked unfavourable criticisms, which, however, were by no means confined to usurious rates, but often extended to any charge whatever for interest. Indeed, the idea that there is some wrong about charging interest for the use of money is not the least remarkable or disastrous, of the various prejudices which have interfered with the happiness and comfort of man. The supposed axiom that *pecunia non parit pecuniam*, the misapplication of certain texts of Scripture, and the supposed interests of the poor, all contributed to the same error. Thus in the reign of Elizabeth (1571) (13 Eliz. cap. 8) an Act was passed against usury and "corrupt chevisance and bargaining by way of sale of wares," which were declared to have abounded, "to the importable hurt of the Common-wealth," declaring usury to be forbidden by the law of God, in its nature sin, and detestable. Quaintly enough, however, this was in the first instance limited to five years, but subsequently (39 Eliz. cap. 18) it was continued on the ground that it was found by experience "to be very necessary and profitable to the Common-wealth of this realm."

---

[1] I have endeavoured to choose the best coin of Cleopatra. But though struck when she was only nineteen, it cannot be said to be very beautiful.

It was for a long time, indeed until the middle of the last century, generally supposed that the rate of interest would, apart from legislative enactment, be regulated by the scarcity or abundance of money; an extraordinary fallacy, when it is considered that the interest itself is payable in money. It is now, however, admitted, by all those who have studied the subject, that the rate of interest, is in the long run, ruled by the average rate of profit derivable from the employment of capital. Of this a striking proof is afforded by the case of Australia, and still more by that of California, where, although, in consequence of their gold mines that metal was peculiarly abundant, the rate of interest has been extremely high. The high rates which prevailed so generally in ancient times were, to a great extent, due to the uncertainty of repayment, both from the unsettled state of politics and from the uncertainty of the laws. I trust I may put in a word for ancient bankers by pointing out that the high rates which they charged were not due to their covetousness, but to this insecurity of repayment. Instead, however, of endeavouring to cure the evil by removing the cause, legislators attempted to put down high rates of interest by rendering them illegal. In this they were not only not successful, but they produced the very opposite effect from that which they intended. Thus, in France the legal rate, which had been 5 per cent., was lowered in 1766 to 4 per cent., but the result was to raise, not to lower the real rate, because the borrower had not only to pay interest, but to compensate the lender for the additional risk.

Again, in Mohammedan countries, notwithstanding

that interest is expressly forbidden in the Koran—or rather, perhaps, to a certain extent, in consequence of that prohibition—the ordinary rate is three or four times as high as in Europe. In England, after the Conquest, as in most other Christian countries at that time, interest was expressly prohibited, both by civil and ecclesiastical law; while, as the Jews were allowed under the Mosaic dispensation to charge interest to strangers, the business of money-lending fell naturally into their hands. Subsequently a similar privilege was accorded to the Italian or Lombard merchants—from whom, of course, Lombard Street, still the centre of banking, derived its name.

In the reign of Henry the Eighth, a statute was passed legalizing interest to the extent of 10 per cent., under James the First it was lowered to 8 per cent., under the Republic to 6 per cent., and in the time of Queen Anne to 5 per cent., and the usury laws were not altogether abolished till 1839. As regards Scotland, interest was altogether illegal until the Reformation. In 1587 it was legalized up to 10 per cent. This Act was repealed in 1552, but revived in 1571, the effect of rendering interest once more illegal having been to raise it from 10 to 14 per cent. Subsequently, in 1633, the legal rate was reduced to 8 per cent., and in 1661, to 6 per cent. In Ireland, interest was forbidden until 1635, when it was legalized up to 10 per cent., reduced in 1704 to 8 per cent., in 1722 to 7 per cent., and in 1732 to 6 per cent. The statute of Anne, above alluded to, applied to the whole kingdom. In 1818, a Committee of the House of Commons was appointed, which reported strongly against the usury laws, but even then so strong

was the popular prejudice that not until 1839 was it
rendered legal to charge a higher rate of discount than
5 per cent.   According to the Code Napoléon, 6 per
cent. was the highest legal rate on commercial loans,
and 5 per cent. on those of real property.   In the
United States, again, the rate is fixed by law, and
varies in the different States, being, for instance, 8
per cent. in Alabama and Texas; 7 per cent. in New
York, South Carolina, Georgia, Michigan, and Wisconsin;
5 per cent. in Louisiana; and 6 per cent. in most of the
other States.   It is unnecessary to say that these re-
strictions are quite inoperative.   It is very remarkable
that so many civilized countries still fail to appreciate
the simple statement of Locke, that "it is in vain to go
about effectually to reduce the price of interest by a law;
and you may as rationally hope to get a fixed rate upon
the hire of houses or ships as of money."

We are generally told in histories of banking, as, for
instance, in that by Gilbart, that the first national bank
was that of Venice, founded in the year 1157, but it
would seem that, as Mr. McLeod has pointed out, this
institution was not at first, in any sense, a true bank.
The state being deeply involved in debt, its creditors
were formed into a corporation and the debts made
transferable like our Consols.   It was not until 1587
that the institution began to take money on deposit.
The depositors received a credit on the bank's books
equal to the actual weight of the bullion placed there,
which the bank undertook to keep intact in its vaults,
and to repay to the depositor at any time, or to transfer
to any one else.

The earliest real bank appears to have been that of

Barcelona, founded in 1401. In this case, the city funds were made responsible for any moneys entrusted to the bank, which not only received deposits, but exchanged money and discounted bills. The Bank of Amsterdam was founded in 1609. The so-called Bank of St. George, at Genoa, dates back to 1407, but does not appear to have done genuine banking business until 1675. The Bank of Stockholm, which commenced in 1668, was the first bank in Europe to issue bank notes, which until that time were totally unknown in the West, although, as we have seen, they had long been in use in China.

Our coinage, however, is far more ancient than our banking system, in so far at least as our present information goes. Our ancestors, before the arrival of the Romans, are generally regarded as mere barbarians. Nevertheless, they were already acquainted with the art of coinage, which, as shown by Mr. Evans in his excellent work on *The Coins of the Ancient Britons*, appears to have commenced in Kent about 200 to 150 B.C., and to have spread over the south-east of England to Devonshire on the west and northwards as far as Yorkshire. The principal mints appear to have been at Camulodunum and Verulamium. The original coins were copies of Gaulish imitations of the staters of Philip of Macedon, which have a head of Apollo on one side and a chariot and horses on the other (Fig. III., Plate II.). Gradually, however, the execution became worse and worse, as shown in the illustrations (Figs. IV., and V., Plate II.), until at length no one looking at one of these coins for the first time would be able to tell which side was meant for the head of Apollo and which for the chariot and horses. The fact that the dies were much larger than the coins assisted in contributing to this result. Some of our coins are inscribed, and in one series we find the name " Cuno " (Fig. VI., Plate II.), short for Cunobeline, the Cymbeline of Shakespeare, from whose name one learned antiquary has absurdly supposed that our word " coin " was derived. Other interesting inscribed coins are those of Commius, supposed to be the Atrebatian mentioned by Cæsar ; of Tincommius and Eppilus the sons of Commius ; of Tasciovanus the father of Cunobeline ; of Dubnovellaunus, probably the Damno Bellaunus of the inscription of Augustus at Ancyra. I ought to add that among the latter coins are various curious types of purely native origin. Nay, not only had the ancient Britons a native coinage, but they were so civilized as to have attained the art of forgery, the false coins being of base metal plated over with gold or silver.

After the conquest the native British coinage was replaced by Roman coins, great numbers of which have been discovered, and some of which are said to be even now occasionally met with in circulation. After the departure of the Romans, the Saxons, about the sixth century, commenced striking stycas, or half-farthings, and sceattas from which comes our proverbial expression " paying one's shot."

Our mode of reckoning by pounds, shillings, and pence, was introduced in Saxon times, the £1 being a pound of silver, though the penny, the $\frac{1}{240}$ of a £1, was the largest silver coin actually struck.

The " penny " is the most ancient representative of our coinage. The name first appears in the laws of Ina, King of the West Saxons, who began to reign in 688.

The figure of Britannia on our present specimens was copied from a coin of Antoninus.

The " mark " was originally Danish, but is said to have been introduced here by Alfred ; it contained at first 100, and afterwards 160 pennies.   It was never struck, but was only a money of account.   Throughout Norman times, the halfpenny and farthing were, as a rule, not separate coins, but halves and quarters of the penny very neatly cut.   Though some Saxon halfpence are known, these coins were not struck in any quantity till the reign of Edward the First.   Our gold coins recommenced under Henry the Third, who coined gold pieces intended to pass for twenty pence.   Edward the Third struck gold florins, current for six shillings.   This coin being found inconvenient, he issued the " noble," sometimes called the " rose noble," worth six shillings and eightpence, or half a mark.   This, with its half and quarters, was our only gold coin, till the " angel " of Edward the Fourth.

Groats and half-groats were introduced by Edward the Third.   They received their name from the French " gros," a large piece.   It was one of the charges against Wolsey that he put his cardinal's hat on the money struck in the archiepiscopal mint at York.   The " shilling," though long used in accounts, was first actually struck by Henry the Eighth.   The silver crown, half-crown, and sixpence commenced under Edward the Sixth.   The sovereign of twenty shillings was first struck by Henry the Seventh.   The guinea commenced under Charles the Second, in 1663, and was so called from the Guinea gold from which it was made ; it was withdrawn in 1815, when the sovereign and half-sovereign were again

issued.   In the middle ages the coinage was constantly
deteriorated by having the edges clipped, now prevented
by the milling of the edge—a process first used in 1560.
The unsatisfactory state of the coin led to the use of
" tradesmen's tokens."

But in addition to the deterioration of the coinage by
wear and by clipping, the standard was gradually reduced by successive sovereigns.   The denomination,
weight and fineness of silver coins have, however, remained unchanged since the time of Elizabeth ; but the
pound sterling, and its relation to the silver coinage, was
not finally fixed until 1717.   Gold was not adopted as
our legal standard of value until 1816.   Silver and
copper, as every one knows, are now " token " coins, and
only legal tender to a limited amount, *i.e.*, the copper
coins up to a shilling, and silver coins to forty shillings.
The so-called " mint price " of silver is 5*s*. 6*d*. an ounce
troy, *i.e.*, the ounce of silver is coined into 5*s*. 6*d*. The
" standard " of silver is 37 parts of silver and 3 of copper.
The quantity of copper and silver coin issued is regulated
by Government according to the supposed requirements
of the country, but any one can take gold to the mint
and have it coined into sovereigns free of expense.
Practically, however, this is never done, because the
Bank of England is always ready to give coin for
bullion, charging 1*d*. an ounce, which is rather less
than the loss of interest which would result from the
time required for coinage.   The sovereign is composed
of 22 parts gold and 2 copper ; most of those now
in circulation are much worn, but when new they
contain 113·001 grains of gold, and weigh 123·274
grains.   An ounce of gold is therefore coined into

£3 17s. 10½d., which is generally termed the mint price of gold.

We sometimes hear surprise expressed that there should be a fixed price for gold. Gold, it is said, should be allowed to follow its market price. But when we are told that the mint price of gold is always £3 17s. 10½d. an ounce, all that is meant is that an ounce of gold is coined into £3 17s. 10½d. The price of gold is fixed in gold, or, in other words, sovereigns are always of the same weight. Sir Robert Peel asked his opponents the well-known question, "What is £1?" and the simple answer is, that £1 is a certain quantity of gold verified by the stamp of the mint.

There appears to be much uncertainty as to when, or by whom, coins were first struck in Ireland and Scotland. As regards the former country, they are never mentioned in the *Senchus Mor*, which is said to have been compiled about A.D. 440, and in which when the precious metals are alluded to, which is but rarely, this is always by weight. Such is indeed the case even to a much later date. Thus in 1004, Brian Boroimhe offered twenty ounces of gold on the altar of St. Patrick at Armagh, though coins are said to have been in use as early as the ninth century. The earliest Scotch coins are supposed to belong to the time of Malcolm the Third, about 1050 A.D.

The derivations of the words relating to money and commerce are interesting and instructive. "Pecuniary" takes us back to the times when value was reckoned by so many head of cattle. The word "money" is from *moneta*, because in Rome coins were first regularly struck in the temple of Juno Moneta, which again was derived from *monere*, to warn, because it was built on the spot where Manlius heard the Gauls approaching to the attack of the city. "Coin" is probably from the Latin word *cuneus*, a die or stamp. Many coins are merely so called from their weight, as for instance our pound, the French livre, Italian lira; others from the metal, as the "aureus"; the "rupee" from the Sanscrit "rupya," silver; others from the design, as the angel, the testoon, from teste, a head; others again from the head of the state, as the sovereign, the crown; others from the name of the monarch, such as the Daric, from Darius, the Philip, Louis d'or, or the Napoleon. The name "obol" was from obeliscus, on account of their form; six making a "drachma" or handful, being as much as the hand could grasp.

The dollar or thaler is short for the Joachimsthaler, or money of the Joachims valley in Bohemia, where these coins were first struck in the sixteenth century. Guineas were called after the country from which the gold was obtained, and the "franc" is an abbreviation of the inscription *Francorum Rex*. The "sou" is from the Latin *solidus*. The word shilling appears to be derived from a root signifying to divide; and in other cases the name indicates the fraction of some larger coin, as the denarius, halfpenny, farthing, cent., and mil. The pound was originally not a coin, but a weight, and comes from the Latin *pondus*. Our pound was originally a pound of silver, which was divided into 240 pennies. The origin of the word penny is unknown. Some have derived it from *pendo*, to weigh, but this does not seem very satisfactory. Our word "sterling" is said to go back to the time of the Conquest, but the derivation has been much disputed. Some have supposed that the name was derived from coins having a star on the obverse, but no coins which could have given rise to such a name are known. The most probable suggestion is that it has reference to the Easterling, or North German merchants.

Early English bankers seem to have been all goldsmiths as well as bankers, and it is, perhaps, just worth mentioning, that in my own firm as in several others, we still use certain books which are specially known as the "Goldsmiths." Sir Walter Bowes, a goldsmith of the sixteenth century, is recorded by Herbert in the history of the Goldsmiths' Company as having lent Henry VIII. £300. Another great goldsmith of this period was Sir T. Gresham, the founder of Gresham College and of the Royal Exchange, which was opened by Queen Elizabeth on January 23rd, 1570. Even Alderman Backwell, who lost £295,994 16s. 6d. when the Exchequer was closed by Charles II., was a retail jeweller, and Pepys records on the 24th December, 1660 : "I went to chuse a payre of candlesticks to be ready for me at Alderman Backewell's." Mr. Price, in his interesting paper on "Early Goldsmiths and Bankers," gives several accounts current appertaining to this period, and still in existence at Messrs. Child's, including for instance one for Prince Rupert for plate, dishes, candlesticks, &c. The oldest of our existing banks are probably Messrs. Child's and Messrs. Martin's. In the reign of Elizabeth there was a goldsmith named John Wheeler, from whom the business passed to William Wheeler, junior, and subsequently into the hands of their apprentices, Messrs. Blanchard and Child, whose names appear in the *Little*

London Directory, 1677. Sir Josiah Child, although he subsequently became a banker himself, attacked our profession with more vigour than common sense in his new *Discourse of Trade*. He says, "This gaining scarcity of money proceeds from the trade of bankering, which obstructs circulation, advances usury, and renders it so easy, that most men, as soon as they can make up a sum of from £50 to £100 send it in to the goldsmith, which doth and will occasion, while it lasts, that fatal pressing necessity for money visible throughout the whole kingdom both to prince and people." Sir Francis Child, called by Pennant the father of the profession, is said to have been the first to lay aside entirely the goldsmith's business and become a pure banker in our sense of the term. The "Grasshopper" in Lombard Street claims to have been the place of business of Sir Thomas Gresham, though his actual residence was in Bishopsgate. In the Directory of 1677, it was occupied by Messrs. Duncombe and Kent, from whom it descended to Messrs. Martin. Hoare's in Fleet Street goes back to James Hore or Hoare, who was Warden of the Mint from 1679 to 1682, and who was probably established in business as early as 1661. They have occupied their present premises since 1692. The Bank of England, I may mention, was founded in 1694.

Although banking, in some form or other, can, as we have seen, be carried back to an early period in history, and even in our own country has long existed, still, in our national accounts, a very archaic system was pursued until quite recently. It is, indeed, scarcely credible that the old wooden "tallies" were only abolished by Mr. Burke's Act, which was passed in 1782, but did not come into full effect till 1826, on the death of the last of the Chamberlains.

The tally was a willow stick, not exceeding five feet in length, about one inch in depth and thickness, with the four sides roughly squared. On one of the four sides the amount was expressed in notches. On each of the two sides next to the notched side the description of the payment was written. The stick was split in half through the notches. One half, constituting the tally, was given to the person making the payment into the Exchequer, the other half, the counter tally, or counterfoil, was kept at the Exchequer as a cheque.

There was no single notch for a larger sum than £1,000; a notch of the gauged width of $1\frac{1}{2}$ inch denoted £1,000; 1 inch £100; $\frac{3}{8}$ inch £10; and half a notch of this last size £1; of $\frac{3}{16}$ inch 1s.; and the smallest notch 1d.; one halfpenny was denoted by a small pounded hole.

In the Return on Public Income and Expenditure, July 29, 1869, the following account is given of the mode in which these tallies were actually issued.

The slip of parchment, or Teller's bill, as it was called, was thrown down a pipe into the Tally court, a large room under the tellers' offices, notice being given to the Tally officer by a clerk calling out "down" through the pipe. The Teller's bill fell upon the large table in the Tally court, which was covered with a chequered cloth. In the Tally court sat officers of the Clerk of the Pells, and of the Auditor as performing the duties of the Chamberlain of the Exchequer. The Teller's bill was first recorded by the officer of the Clerk of the Pells, in his book of *introitus* or receipt, and then passed over to

the Auditor's clerk, who entered it into a book called
the bill of the day. A copy of each Teller's bill was
written by the Auditor's clerk upon an indented form
of receipt (up to 1826 upon the wooden tally, the amount
being expressed in notches only), and given upon his
application, generally on the following day, to the re-
ceiver or other person paying in the money. At the
close of the day, when all the Tellers' bills had been
sent down and entered, the bill of the day was sent
on to the clerk of the cash-book, in which book all the
receipts of the day were entered. The Auditor's cash-
book was the foundation of all the accounts of the
receipt of revenue, weekly, quarterly, and yearly
certificates of which were transmitted from the Exchequer to the Treasury, from which the annual
accounts of revenue were prepared and laid before
Parliament.

In early days our bankers and merchants used to
deposit their superfluous cash in the Tower of London
for safe keeping. Charles I. seized the money there,
amounting to £120,000. A still more serious misfortune befell our predecessors however, in 1672, when the
Exchequer was closed by Charles II., at the instance of
Lord Ashley and Sir Thomas Clifford, and when the
amount seized was no less than £1,328,000. The first
"run" on record took place when the Dutch fleet sailed
up the Thames, burned Chatham, and destroyed Sheer-
ness. I have already alluded to the fact that such
references to bankers as appear in ancient literature are
far from being always of a complimentary character ;
such is also the case even in recent times. Lord Eldon
is reported to have selected his bankers by a sort of

inverse competitive examination. He thought them the stupidest in London, and he said that if he could find stupider, he would move his account. And it is no doubt true that probity and prudence, tact and knowledge of human nature, are more necessary to a banker than the possession of great genius. It is, perhaps, natural that I should be disposed to attribute the unfavourable remarks to which I have referred rather to jealousy than to conviction.

We may, I think, congratulate ourselves that we have contributed our fair share to those who have successfully laboured to promote the welfare of the country. In political life, innumerable bankers have been useful members of the legislature. In some cases, our banking families have held high office. In literature, the honoured name of Grote at once suggests itself, and in science I may be permitted to mention my own father. One might have supposed that banking was rather too prosaic for poetry, but the names of Rogers, Wright, and Praed prove the contrary. Among economists we have Lord Overstone, Mr. Norman, Mr. Bagehot, Mr. Hankey, Mr. Newmarch, Mr. Palgrave, and others too numerous to mention. Indeed, though I am by no means a follower of M. Comte, there is one of his proposals which has much to recommend it. He suggests, in the *Catéchisme Positiviste*, that the supreme government in each country should be entrusted to three bankers, who would respectively take charge of commercial, manufacturing, and agricultural operations. " A ces triumvirs," he says, " le sacerdoce occidental, dirigé par le Grand-Prêtre de l'humanité, devra dignement soumettre les réclamations légitimes d'un immense prolétariat." I should have been disposed to think that, at any rate, such a government would have had the great merit of doing its best to preserve the peace of the world, though I confess that of late some of my friends have developed a fierce military spirit, which fills me with astonishment. But, however that may be, I think we may fairly claim for the banking profession, that they have done their best to deserve the confidence reposed in them. Let us hope the opportunities and advantages which will be afforded by the Bankers' Institute will be a benefit to the profession, by extending a knowledge of the true principles of banking, and even perhaps to the public, by tending to remove those groundless apprehensions which from time to time, as for instance last year, have produced an entirely artificial stringency in the money market, and an elevation of the rate of interest quite unnecessary in itself, and very prejudicial to the commerce of the country.

I cannot conclude without mentioning another class of banks, namely, the Savings Banks, which have done so much to promote frugality among the poorer classes of the community. The original idea seems due to the Rev. Josiah Smith of Wendover, who in 1799, in conjunction with some of his neighbours, arranged to receive small sums from the parishioners during the summer, repayable on demand, but to which he added a bonus if the balance remained until Christmas. The next Savings Bank, that founded at Tottenham by Mrs. Priscilla Wakefield, in 1804, more nearly resembled our existing Savings Banks.

But, gentlemen, I must not abuse the privilege of " unlimited issue," which your kindness has accorded to me.   I remember one of our country friends, disturbed, I suppose, at the moment of writing, drew a bill on us once for 180 years, instead of, no doubt, for £180. I wish that by any reasonable expenditure on our parts, that we could have secured such a term of life to him.   But I fear if I continue to enlarge on the theme which I have selected, tempting and inexhaustible as it is, you may be driven to organize a "run."   To prevent so unpleasant a result, I will now conclude; thanking you once more for the great honour conferred on me in electing me as the first President of the Institute of Bankers.

THE END.